GW00362933

RIDING MADLY OFF
IN ALL DIRECTIONS

Riding Madly Off
In All Directions

by

RONALD BELL

Lord Ronald . . . flung himself upon his horse
and rode madly off in all directions

Stephen Leacock,
Nonsense Novels: Gertrude the Governess

The Memoir Club

© Ronald Bell 2001

First published in 2001 by
The Memoir Club
Whitworth Hall
Spennymoor
County Durham

All rights reserved.
Unauthorised duplication
contravenes existing laws.

British Library Cataloguing in
Publication Data.
A catalogue record for this book
is available from the
British Library.

ISBN: 1 84104 020-7

Typeset by George Wishart & Associates, Whitley Bay.
Printed by Bookcraft (Bath) Ltd.

I dedicate this book with deepest love and gratitude to

Eva Margaret Bell, née Cranshaw,

My sweetheart, wife, mother of my children
Nicolette and Philip, and adored
Grandma to Marcel and Pascal Porcheron.

My wife at nineteen.

Contents

Part VII – Political and Social Comment

List of Illustrations

Acknowledgements

As I have travelled the long road of my life, the following key figures have served as 'milestones', guiding me on my way to a happy retirement:-

My godfather, Charles Howard Rainey; my teacher at Rotherhithe Nautical School, J.S. Stead; Dr. Kempling FRCO, the Choirmaster at St. John the Divine, Kennington; CPO G. Avenal RN, my instructor in HMS *Ganges*; Jack Jarvis, A. Archer, R. Dockerill and C.H. Thomas (Managing Director), all of EMI.

Robert Reisdorff (Managing Director), Lee Mendell, International Director, Liberty Records; Martin Davis, Managing Director, United Artists Records; Frau Barbara Hildebrandt-Körber, UA Records, Hamburg; Al Bennett, President, Liberty Records; Cliff Busby, EMI; Yeoman of Signals J. Fisher, RN; my brother Billy. Finally I must not forget that unknown Drafting Commander RN who removed me from the tragic carrier, HMS *Courageous*, just before she sailed for her fateful encounter with U29.

Without the patience, understanding and great kindness of these in particular, I would today be a sad and lonely man.

Preface

This book is based upon the 'grasshopper' principle. It has no narrative, no logical succession of events, and it jumps from one decade to another, from country to country, and channels a stream of consciousness recalling people, places and episodes from my perhaps unusual life.

It might be useful to travellers in planes or trains, and for those imprisoned in airport lounges or railway stations. It might even serve as a way of escape from fellow passengers on cruise liners!

The lines quoted from Stephen Leacock's Nonsense Novel, *Gertrude the Governess*, which have been quoted on the title page, describe perfectly how I approached the format of this book: 'Ronald said nothing. He flung himself from the room, flung himself upon his horse, and rode madly off in all directions.'

I could not have completed the book without the sustained support and fine professionalism of Miss Chantal Bowen. Whether Chantal deserves praise or censure, only our readers can decide.

Every man, it is said, has a book in him. My readers may derive comfort from the fact that I shall never write another! For a two-fingered typist and poor speller it was drudgery. Thank heavens for Tippex!

Ronald Bell

PART 1

Family Life

CHAPTER 1

My Parents

Today is our father's birthday. I always think about him on this day, reflecting on the hard life he had. In the lottery of this life he drew bad cards; the main elements of his time in this world were unemployment in the post-World War I world and, of course, the War itself. Passchendaele and Ypres seared the souls of all those who took part in those blood-soaked infantry battles. Yet in one regard our father was lucky; he found the perfect wife.

Our mother, née Daisy Bradley, became, like the girl in the song who rode a bicycle made for two – Daisy Bell! I used to chuckle at how one so small as she could control one so big as our dad. In marriage it is surely rare to find a man always so eager to spend every possible moment with his wife. Our father used to hurry home to her and, when working, would hand over his wage packet to her unopened. He never willingly went anywhere without her. Our mama spent many an hour in the *Crown & Anchor*, the *Black Horse*, the *Live & Let Live* and other Brixton (London) pubs. She would rather have been at home but he always wanted her to be with him when he sank his pints. I used to wonder where he put all that beer and thought he must have hollow legs. Yet he never got drunk or caused any trouble through his drinking; he knew his capacity. It was enough to make a sailor jealous!

He was only fifty-six when he died, but at least he died in the knowledge that my brother William and I had both found sweet wives and he did have that unique and precious human experience of holding a grandson and a granddaughter in his arms.

CHAPTER 2

My Mother

My mother had died. She was 88 years old and a very funny old lady. She considered all Americans to be either cowboys or gangsters! We should remember that she grew up in a time when Great Britain was the greatest power on earth. Our school maps showed vast areas of the world coloured red, the colour denoting the British Empire.

So, although a most kindly soul, she viewed people from other nations with some suspicion. They were 'foreigners' and did not belong among us. When my brother wrote from America to tell us that he was taking out American citizenship, she was annoyed and thought him guilty of some kind of treason! It took several years and the arrival of American grandchildren before she relented and forgave him.

Just before her death, the matron of the old folks' hospital called me into her office and said: 'You had better have a word with your mother, for last night she attacked one of our old gentlemen patients'. 'Good heavens,' I exclaimed, 'Why ever did she do that?' (As I have said, she was ever the very soul of human kindness.) It transpired that the gentleman, one of only four male patients in a small side ward, had ventured into the Green Room, overlooking the fact that this housed the TV and was a room taken over by the old ladies and regarded by them as their private sanctum for gossiping and watching TV.

For his intrusion the poor fellow was awarded a severe clip around the ear! He failed to observe the unwritten rule that the Green Room was a 'no go' area for male patients. I took my naughty old mama to task, but she said that the old chap had no business in there and it served him right! No good arguing with her!

I see her now, my mother, racing another old lady down the corridor, both using their 'walking frames'. On fine days she would urge me to go faster and faster, racing other old ladies in their push chairs around the hospital grounds – a kind of geriatric Le Mans! Just imagine! This jolly old lady used to cradle me in her arms during the Zeppelin air raids on London during World War I. We sheltered under the stairs like many others.

In World War II she worried about me again, but much more about my brother William, also a sailor, but in his case with a very distinguished war

My mother with the author and Tom Griffiths.

record. He was aboard the famous old battleship HMS *Warspite* when she was exposed to deadly air attacks by the Luftwaffe inside the confined waters of the Norwegian fjord at Narvic, where *Warspite* sank several German destroyers. Later this ship flew the flag of Admiral Cunningham, C. in C. Mediterranean, whose ships engaged the Italian fleet at Matapan and effectively ended the Italian naval presence in those waters. Brother Billy also served in MTB's in the English Channel and, after a short encounter with a superior German force, returned to harbour with several dead, though Billy, like me of small stature, was unscathed.

For my part there is no doubt that I had a personal guardian angel. Nearly all the ships I served on were sunk but never with me on board. My last ship was the carrier HMS *Courageous*, sunk by U29 early in the War. Four hundred of my shipmates were lost on that dreadful day. On shore at the time I felt empty and miserable when I heard of her loss.

The Devil, says my wife, looks after his own!

CHAPTER 3

My Father, Victim of World War I

Mother and I took the old red London bus from Brixton to Clapham Junction, thence to Richmond. My father was recovering from a War illness of a nervous nature. These frequent visits to the famous Army Hospital at Netley, near Richmond, were a feature of our lives until his release around 1927. A Royal Engineer attached to the Guards Division, he shared the ordeal of those brave men who marched from the Channel ports through France and Belgium via Ypres and Passchendaele to Cologne. I remember how my father used sometimes to ruffle my hair and smile at me as he chatted to Mother. I understood it not at the time, but he must have been very ill and I treasure today a picture of the men in his ward. They had gaunt, haunted faces, some staring at the world with eyes which seemed unable to accept or recognise any more of its mindless cruelty.

At home, my mother was often in tears and I did not understand why. After his death, my father left some postcards sent to Mother from the front. He also left some terrible souvenirs taken from a dead German soldier, including his infantry manual, his German soldier's song book, and other tattered and worn memorabilia. To this day they offer dreadful and poignant testimony, especially when one looks around the present-day world and realises that nothing has changed. Bosnia and Africa bear witness to this fact, to name but two of the many conflicts still raging.

Here is a First World War soldiers' song which Father used to sing to us when he had drunk a pint or two of strong ale:

> We haven't seen the Kaiser for a hellova time,
> Hellova time,
> He's been blown up by a mine!
> He's the leader of the German gang,
> Gott strafe him, he's no cousin of mine!

It was a World War I marching song which was very popular with the men of the British Expeditionary Force. The Kaiser had called them 'a contemptible little army'. He is also alleged to have made the following remark about that same B.E.F.: 'We will leave them with nothing but their eyes to weep with!'

My parents, 1917, and the author in petticoats!

CHAPTER 4

My Father and George V

My Mother used to tell my brother and me the following true story about our father and the King of England, George V. One day the King visited the Netley Hospital for ex-soldiers in Richmond, Surrey, presumably to commiserate with World War I patients, all sufferers from the Front Line. These war-torn men were standing by their beds as His Majesty entered the ward accompanied by the Matron (a formidable lady). According to Mother, the King asked my father how he was and Father replied (to the horror of the Matron, who hissed, 'Be quiet, Bell'): 'Well, Your Majesty, a packet of Woodbines and a current bun will not solve my problems!' I like to believe this story, for it was typical of our father, who never minced words. (For younger readers, Woodbines, five for a penny, were very cheap and very popular cigarettes right up to World War II.)

CHAPTER 5

Father and Fred, the Cat's Meat Man

Although not born within the sound of Bow Bells, my father was a typical Londoner with a quirky sense of humour, very like that of Berliners. Citizens of both these once proud imperial cities share a love of jokes made at the expense of the less fortunate of this world.

Fred, the catsmeat man, was one of these poor souls. He drew a bad hand in the lottery of life, for he was of short stature, frail of physique, wore heavy rimmed spectacles and was of low intelligence. For these limitations he was compensated by possessing a sweet nature that endeared him to his many customers.

Fred called twice a week and became very friendly with my father. He always stopped for a cup of tea and my naughty father used to say, 'Fred, will you pop over the road and fetch me a packet of Woodbines?' Fred never refused, and whilst he was away, my father used to lift our cat Ben and place him in the wicker basket, where, for the next ten minutes or so, our cat lived the life of a feline Henry VIII. It was a gargantuan feast indeed! It was both sad and comic to see how Fred never seemed to notice how his stock had diminished, or notice that lucky black cat lying prostrate and helpless with bulging belly!

Our mother, I suspect, used to recompense Fred. She was always cross with Father about him.

CHAPTER 6

Father and the Drumset

At school I bought a drum set consisting of a big drum, a side drum and cymbals, transported home with the help of my school friend, Jimmy Mullinder. I paid him a shilling! My parents were aghast at the prospect of some very noisy evenings. At first they told me to take it back but my pleas prevailed and we kept the drums.

A couple of days later Jimmy Mullinder appeared at our front door with a note from his father demanding the return of the set. The following dialogue ensued.

Father: 'Hello Jimmy, what can we do for you?' 'I've got a letter for you, Sir', said Jimmy. Father opened it and said, 'Jimmy, is your father bigger than me?' 'No Sir,' said my friend. 'Well go back home and tell your dad that you can't have the drums back!' Jimmy's dad did not rise to the challenge and we kept the drums, which became a source of great disturbance; I could use them only when Father was out.

Retribution followed that Christmas when we had a party and Mrs Breden, a lodger, imbibed unwisely and fell into the big drum. So that is how the jazz world lost a great drummer!

CHAPTER 7

My Wife Peggy

Following a minor domestic misdemeanour, a rapid exchange of fire took place between my sweet wife Peggy and myself. A ceasefire has been agreed so I can leave my bedroom bunker. After fifty-eight years of marriage, we NEVER quarrel about important matters; it is the little things – 'these foolish things' – that can start a conflagration. My Peggy is a perfectionist; things must be done properly, one must be clean and tidy... not leave undone that which should be done... or else! Doors left open, crumbs on the carpet, clothing left lying about, or forgetting to clean the bath after use – these are the misdeeds that can upset a very lovely and incomparable lady. A wonderful sweetheart, a marvellous wife and utterly dedicated mother and now... an adored grandma. A lucky man am I!

CHAPTER 8

Peggy's Grandparents

[The following account was contributed by my wife Peggy, née Cranshaw]

My grandmother (maternal) was a staunch Church of England lady, who, strangely, married a staunch Roman Catholic! It was always a wonder to the family that they had a large family and stayed married for all their lives. Thursday afternoon was sacrosanct to Rose Maria; she always had the curate to visit her.

Grandfather, of course, was aware of the young man's love of duty to his Church in visiting this elderly lady, who found it difficult to get about and could not attend church.

My grandfather was gardener to a Mrs Press (her husband owned a well known company who did road repairs), and he finished his work in time to arrive home before the arrival of the curate.

Having worked hard from early morning with just a break for lunch, he was naturally relieved to be able to sit back in his armchair and rest a while. Grandmother had other views. Her husband, still in his working clothes although with hands and face washed, was not, in her opinion, fit to be seen by the curate!

She herself, naturally, was by this time bathed, adorned in her best dress, with hair well brushed – even a little powder on her face, and anxious that her husband should vacate the room before the curate should be faced by an artisan who was not in his best clothes.

The next horror was the fact that time was rushing by; there was only about ten minutes left and Grandfather was in no hurry whatsoever to rise from his chair. If she looked at the clock once, she looked a dozen times. Still he sat there and, to crown it all, he said, 'Don't they give their ministers any food at that vicarage? They always come at a mealtime!' He looked at the clock – again! Stretching his arms above his head, he said, 'Oh well, I suppose I had better go upstairs'. The clock stood at a minute or two to four o'clock. He rose, proceeded to the stairs and went up. The bell rang and Grandmother's guest had arrived. Her ordeal of nerves was over!

Grandpa wrote this impertinent but amusing piece of doggerel for his wife, Rose Maria:-

13

Rose Maria sat on the fire.
The fire was too hot, she sat on the pot.
The pot was too round, she sat on the ground.
The ground was too flat, she sat on the cat.
And the cat ran away with Maria on its back!

CHAPTER 9

The Wedding

What a fortunate young woman was my wife Peggy on that day in 1939 when she met me! She was fortunate on three counts: first, because a sailor of the Royal Navy consented to marry her; second, because that sailor was a *Ganges* boy; and last, but certainly not least, because that sailor was me – Ronald Bell, a signalman TO D/JX136327.

'I don't want to go out with a sailor,' she said when I suggested we should go out together so that I could assess her suitability as my regular girlfriend. Overlooking this slight against the finest body of men riding the oceans of the world, I took her to the pictures and spent a wonderfully romantic evening in the rear seats at the cost of two shillings and three pence each . . . a grievous loss of beer money! I told her I considered her satisfactory and that she would do for my sweetheart. Some two years later, on August 8th 1942, I arranged to marry her. A momentous, an unforgettable day!

My bride's father was a dear Lancastrian and her mother an equally dear lady from the county of Kent.

They guarded their daughter's honour with a strict but kind surveillance and during my trips up the line from Guzz (Devonport), she had to be home by 2230 hours and her dad would be waiting at her garden gate. A kindly soul, he would discreetly vanish indoors as we said goodnight. (It took, in those days, about a week before I got my first kiss!)

But, how nervous was her father on the wedding day! I think he was afraid I might change my mind. He proffered me a cigarette almost every five minutes and plied me with cups of tea. Feeling not unlike a condemned man heading for the scaffold, I found myself at last waiting in my pew for my bride to arrive. At this point the vicar, who had several ceremonies to perform that day, said rather tartly: 'Shall we begin?' 'Hang on a minute, Vicar,' I said, 'Can I have a quick last look around just to make sure there is nothing better?' There was not, nor could there ever have been another bride so lovely as she glided down the aisle on the arm of her father; the organ swelled with Mendelssohn's *Wedding March* and so did my heart. I can never forget the wonder of her shy smile through her white veil and, as she stood beside me, I understood for a moment the holy

Our wedding – the most wonderful day.

significance of the marriage sacrament. After the ceremony we retired to the vestry to sign the documents and to remunerate the vicar with the then customary seven shillings and sixpence! He took one look at my bride and gave me five shillings change! (NOT true!)

Now, more than fifty-eight years later, I look at my still lovely seventy-eight year old wife and my heart skips a beat. We have been through as many trials and hassles as most and I suspect that her main interests these days are our two delightful grandsons, yet I confess, it was *I* who was so lucky on that far-off day in 1939!

NB: I had hair and teeth in those days.

CHAPTER 10

Peggy's 'A' Level

It is night and as my lady lies beside me, we both stare up at the ceiling. She is restless, tossing and turning so that I begin to wonder whether we are at sea in a force ten gale. There is tension in the air; I sense trouble brewing as sleep defies us both.

The cause of this unease? Ah – suddenly it dawns upon me! Early this morning the postman delivered an official envelope containing my lady's long-awaited 'A' Level result. I suspect that the result has not been one to give satisfaction. After several months' twice-weekly attendance at night school for studies in English Literature, as well as intense study of several set books, my wife Peggy has failed the exam! The night school attendances were shared with her friend pursuing the same English course. I have gathered from an unusually long telephone conversation with her friend that my Peggy has been the recipient of very unwelcome condolences. Her friend *passed*!

Now here it is that my naval sense of humour takes charge of our bedtime odyssey and things rapidly deteriorate to a stormy half hour! Sailors enjoy the misfortunes of others, although traditionally ever chivalrous and quick to aid the unfortunate.

Trying both to mollify and to aggravate at the same time, I remark: 'Never mind, love, you are the only lady in Highview Road with two 'O' Levels! (A failed 'A' award is the equivalent of an 'O' Level grade. Peggy already has an 'O' Level). 'Oh shut up!' she says, becoming slowly riled. We continue looking up at the ceiling and I sense a tidal wave of bitter disappointment engulfing my unhappy wife. Those naval leprechauns urge me on to further provocation. After a pause I remark: 'Well, for the life of me I can't understand why you failed. Another pause and I continue: 'You read all the set books and your teacher told you he was confident that you would succeed . . . and I know you worked hard; I had to wait for my dinner on Tuesdays and Thursdays'. (By now I am aware that the pot of disappointment is boiling in earnest!) Another pause . . . then I deliver the coup de grâce! 'Which Shakespeare play was one of your set books?' I enquire with feigned concern. *'As you like It,'* answers Peggy. 'That's funny,' say I, 'I thought I saw you reading *Romeo and Juliet.' All hell breaks loose!* The bed rocks and my Peggy leaps about a foot in the air. Then she, who *never* uses bad language, says: '*Shut up about the* **#*#*#*g** 'A' Level!!!' Sometimes I wish I had been in the Air Force!

Next morning we both laugh . . . but I notice a certain coolness in Peggy's relationship with the friend who has passed . . . Women!

CHAPTER 11

Husbands

For 58 years my sweet wife Peggy has endured my male chauvinist homilies. The other evening I concluded one such by remarking that women who were not fortunate enough to have a man usually kept a dog instead! 'Ah, yes,' said Peggy, 'But what's the difference?'

CHAPTER 12

Peggy's 'Put-Down'

The TV is off! She looks at me, I look at her and I wonder who will break the silence of this lonely village night. Nostalgia for our long-lost youth puts me into a romantic mood and I ask her: 'Why did you choose me?' 'I can't remember,' says my cheeky wife. Somewhat put down by her reply, I try again to awaken a sentimental and ego-flattering response. 'Well,' I say, 'There must have been something for you to choose me when London was agog with American GIs, Free French and Polish soldiers . . . Was it my bell-bottom trousers?' 'No,' she said, and then I remember what almost her first words to me were: 'I don't want to go out with a sailor.'

I try another angle. 'Was it because I had animal magnetism like Errol Flynn?' She almost falls off her chair with laughing. At this point I feel it best to let the matter drop.

Lord Byron said, 'Marriage is not a bed of roses, but a field of battle'. Amen to that!

In nearly sixty years, my wonderful wife, adored mother and grandma, has struck me a blow three times. That works out a clout every twenty years! I am due for the next one in March 2002!

CHAPTER 13

The Intruder

Good God! Tumult below! A burglar? I rise from my afternoon slumber to hear my wife yelling: 'Ron, Ron, Ron – come quickly!'

Arming myself with a vase and advancing with (very considerable) trepidation, I descend the stairs prepared to rescue my frightened lady. I find her cowering in a corner of the lounge. Meanwhile a large bird (he must have come down the chimney) is swooping around the room like a Spitfire from World War II.

Now I assume the role of problem-solver. Feeling not unlike Sir Galahad himself, I take command of the situation and, in a voice like an RN Gunnery Officer's about to shout 'FIRE!' to his twin six-inch guns, I say: 'Go into the kitchen and bring me the washing-up bowl and tea tray. Hurry!'

My lady returns with these implements and hands them to me. Waiting until the bird alights on the window sill, I move in swiftly to enclose him in the bowl and hold him fast against the wall, whilst slowly edging the tray in so as to enclose him completely.

Another crisp RN command: 'Open the kitchen door!' Then, bearing our imprisoned intruder, I hurry through it to the garden beyond. There I release him and watch him fly off in a great flurry. As he flies, I am prepared to swear that he shrieks 'Thank you, thank you!' before making his final exit.

My lady makes a pot of tea. 'My hero!' she says.

I cannot help feeling grateful to that ornithological intruder. He has made my day!

CHAPTER 14

Rotherhithe Nautical School

There was a Nautical Training School in the twenties run by the London County Council in Rotherhithe, South East London. I attended this excellent school, which taught ordinary London boys such diverse subjects as Maths, Navigation, English, History and Seamanship.

We were taught to do knots and splices and to wash ourselves and be smart and seaman-like in behaviour. How proud I was when I donned my first bell-bottoms! I rolled along the streets of Rotherhithe, Bermondsey and Brixton, where I lived, as if I had just come through a force ten gale. Each Wednesday we went to Surrey Docks for boat pulling and sailing. In those days our young eyes were thrilled to see the forest of masts of merchantmen from all over the world. The tang of the sea assailed our nostrils and we all longed to board ship and set off for distant foreign lands.

It was our custom to march from the school to the docks, each boy carrying, in a vertical position, an oar. For a rather small boy such as I was, keeping the oar upright was somewhat difficult and on one occasion as we traversed Rotherhithe New Road, the oar took charge. I could not hold it and it swung wildly away from me, sweeping some of the other boys' oars in its path.

The resulting chaos did not just hold up the traffic as we reorganised ourselves; it also brought upon my head the wrath of Captain J. Weekes, our instructor, who seemed to feel I had humiliated the entire school. A retired Master Mariner, small and bearded, we boys loved and feared him. His favourite term of rebuke was, 'You damned hound!' He was a marvellous man and one who is remembered with great respect by all who came under his sway.

On another occasion I earned a rope's end, and a 'damned hound' verbal lashing occurred during a knots and splices lesson. We gathered in a circle round the Captain, all seated on our haunches, as he demonstrated the intricacies of making a Turk's Head. All heads bent over his deft fingers. The Captain had a bald patch in the middle of his head and one mischievous imp (me!), whilst apparently intent upon watching the proceedings, tickled the Captain's bald patch with a few strands of yarn. At first the dear old chap did not suspect that it was anything but an itinerant fly irritating his

My classmates at the LCC Nautical School, Rotherhithe.
The author, second row left, second one up.

pate. I repeated the tickling whilst leaning over his shoulder, apparently absorbed in that Turk's Head knot. It was not until he had been sorely tried that our instructor suddenly realised who and what it was that was tormenting him. 'You damned hound!' he roared, seizing a rope's end and lashing out as I fled the class. It took several days before I was forgiven and when I related this prank to my mother, she was not pleased. 'You apologise', she said, and I did.

One wonders what awful consequences would have befallen Captain Weekes for chasing and walloping a naughty boy in today's sick, politically correct, society.

CHAPTER 15

Captain Weekes and the Mast

On one occasion dear old retired sea dog, Captain Weekes was our seamanship instructor and was teaching us how to use a bos'n's chair with a block and tackle.

The object of the lesson was to hoist the Captain to the top of the mast situated in the school playground and to teach us how, by controlling a rope passing through a block at the top of the mast, we could hoist or lower someone in the bos'n's chair.

If the passage aloft and down again was to be accomplished safely, everything depended on a strict control of the rope holding the chair. The speed of the chair was in turn dependent upon the boy holding the rope, which had a couple of turns around a cleat fixed to the mast.

Unfortunately for Captain Weekes, the boy on the rope was ME.

From the top of the mast the Captain shouted, 'Lower away!'

Instead of paying out the rope slowly, thus ensuring an orderly descent, I let the rope run through my hands at a fast rate, with the result that Captain Weekes returned to earth like a meteor! 'You damned hound,' said the Captain, not for the first time.

It was that rope's end again for me – and well deserved!

CHAPTER 16

Choirboy Pranks at St John the Divine

From the age of seven, until fourteen I was a choirboy in the lovely South London church of St John The Divine, Kennington. In the twenties and thirties, St John's choir was acclaimed as one of the finest in London. We were sometimes invited to sing in Southwark Cathedral. Our rivals were the celebrated All Saint's, Margaret Street and the Temple Church in Central London, who were singularly lucky to have the treble voice of Ernest Lough. His recordings of *Hear my Prayer* and *Oh for the wings of a Dove* went around the world and remain today one of the glories of the whole history of recorded music.

Despite my presence, St John's choir was numbered among the élite. The services on Sunday evenings attracted large congregations; in those days people went to church! These Sunday services always included a lengthy sermon and it was known that unless provided with alternative distractions, some twenty choirboys would fidget and become restless.

To counter this we were allowed to read books during sermons. Among our favourites were adventure books by writers such as G.A. Henty, whose stories were laced with patriotic tales of fierce fighting against rebellious natives in distant parts of the Empire. Brave soldiers triumphed over stupendous odds; our mission was to bring law and order to the native peoples. No wonder no one reads G.A. Henty today!

One Sunday I felt the need for excitement during the sermon. Under my surplice I had paper pellets and a catapult with strong elastic. My target was dear old Canon Down, a venerable old cleric, the erudition of whose sermons was often far above the heads of the long-suffering congregation. On this occasion I, apparently absorbed in G.A. Henty, took careful aim and scored a direct hit on Father Down. He appeared to ignore this attack so a few moments later I fired another pellet. Again no response, but after the service he beckoned me to follow him into the sacristy where the clergy attired themselves in their vestments and disrobed after services. 'Ronald,' said Father Down, 'you are an extremely naughty boy and I shall write to your parents to ask them to withdraw you from the choir.'

I walked home feeling much like Sir Walter Raleigh the night before his execution. My father, a devout churchman and devotee of choral

The author at fourteen in Cambridge.

music, would, I knew, react drastically to the news of my dismissal in disgrace.

When I told her, my mother said: 'Oh dear, now you are in for it'. She was right. My father was a dear good man, but a bit of a Prussian in disciplinary matters.

Soon after this incident my voice broke and dear Father Down forgave me and allowed me to return and assist at Mass as an acolyte. Father forgave me too.

Today the church, with its fine steeple, still dominates the area around the end of the Brixton Road and the Oval, Kennington. But the choir stalls are gone and stacked forlornly in the Lady Chapel. The pews are reduced by about a third from what they were long ago. On a recent visit I saw ghosts . . . I saw my fellow choirboys emerging in pairs from the vestry, taking the short walk to the chancel gate, where we used to separate into *cantori decani* choir stalls. I heard again the great organ played by our dedicated musician and teacher, Dr Kempling, and I heard once more the rich basses, altos and tenors of that splendid assembly of lovely voices.

Alas, the High Altar, the centre stage for the mystery of the Mass, is no longer in use and a smaller altar, situated at the chancel gate, replaces it. It was all too sad; I fled.

I knew it not as a boy, but how blessed were we to have come under the influence of the late Dr Kempling FRCO. With infinite patience he taught us to phrase and understand the words we were singing. He saved me from being a moron!

Dr Kempling brought great music into my life and enriched me and my fellows beyond measure. Beethoven, the Bachs, Mozart, Schuman, Schubert, Fauré and Mendelssohn and many others endowed our young hearts with an appreciation of beauty that is with us today. What a treasure house are the *English Hymnal*, *Hymns Ancient and Modern*, the anthems of Walford Davis, Sir John Goss, John Stainer, Vaughan Williams and Sir Edward Elgar, as well as others too numerous to mention!

I believe Dr Kempling is in Paradise and playing the organ and training the angels in a great celestial cathedral.

> 'He is a portion of the loveliness
> Which once he made more lovely'
>
> *Percy Bysshe Shelley*

CHAPTER 17

Sex!

George Mikes, an anglicised Greek, well known for his book about the English, wrote the following:-

'Continental people have a sex life; the English have hot water bottles!'

This is a libel! I found out about sex one lovely July day when I was just coming up to fourteen years. It was in the Doctor's garden in Brixton, where my parents kept house. In that garden stood two large beech trees with a splendid spread of branches.

One evening one of the rather pretty girls next door called Alma (her Father was the Registrar of Births, Marriages and Deaths for Lambeth), wanted to show she was equal to any boy in climbing. Up through the leafy labyrinth she followed me to a place where the branches formed a kind of natural seat for two. As we sat there for some moments, we both became aware that the sun was setting and that our tree was bathed in soft light. Alma was about eighteen and had always treated me with that infuriating contempt that girls reserve for younger boys. Now, however, we were both suddenly filled with a kind of awareness; it was a magical, reverential feeling that drew our two selves closer. The sun's beams were like gold dust between the leaves and branches and it was all so still and beautiful.

Suddenly she bent forward and pulled my head towards her. Her lips, rosy red and moist, sent a million volts through my shivering form as her lips touched mine. Oh the divine Alma! With a mocking laugh she clambered down the tree and was away. I can still hear the rustle of her summer dress and the tantalising sound of her voice.

Alma made me realise just how interesting girls were. Hitherto I had had no interest whatsoever in the soppy creatures. Today, I still look at girls; alas, they do not look at me! I still have occasional, non-romantic encounters with them on the buses. Now and again, in the rush hour when the buses are crowded, some young thing will stand up and offer me a seat (never the young men)!

CHAPTER 18

Edwardian Days

In my early boyhood, at the beginning of the '20's, there was neither radio nor television and home entertainment, if any, was available only if there was sufficient talent in a family to provide it.

Many homes had a piano or a concertina, some a violin, but it was mainly a combination of the piano with voices that helped to pass away long winter evenings.

In suburbia, family sing-songs were common, but in the more refined houses they held soirées in the drawing room

At our large house in the Brixton Road, where my parents were caretakers, Charles Rainey, a pioneer physiotherapist, held periodical soirées in his elegant drawing room with lush curtains, period furniture and a Broadwood piano, which seemed to dominate the room as it shone brightly in the light of a beautiful chandelier high up in the ceiling. The thick-pile, wine-red carpet supported a flower-decked chintz-covered sofa and chairs.

Charles Rainey, held in low esteem by doctors, was a man of culture and he specialised in doctors' 'failures'. He had much success. His soirées reflected his good taste and he was admired by many friends; invitations to his soirées were accepted with alacrity.

Among his regular guests were Mr and Mrs Oyler from Tunbridge Wells in Kent. Mr Oyler, a schools inspector, was a former patient. His wife, a well-rounded matron, was always clad in highly coloured dresses and wore bracelets, prominent earrings and rather gaudy necklaces. Despite this sartorial ostentation, she was an extremely kind woman, especially to my brother Billy and me.

Mrs Oyler enjoyed singing and seemed unaware of the fact that she was a poorly endowed contralto with a weak upper register. Sometimes 'as a treat', Billy and I, wearing our best suits, were allowed into the drawing room to hear Mrs Oyler sing. Our mother told us to be good boys and so we sat captive, whilst Mrs Oyler rendered such 'hits' from the Edwardian hit parade as *Believe me if all those endearing young charms*, *Because*, *Drink to me only with thine eyes* and *The Indian Love Call* by Amy Woodforde Finden. We soon became restless, especially when Mrs Oyler reached – in vain – for the higher notes of the musical scale. As her stress increased, so did ours.

It made us think someone was killing a cat! It ended usually with us both being ejected from that drawing room. Such rooms, such songs have slipped out of all our lives.

One evening when Mrs Oyler was in full throat, so that the chandelier seemed to vibrate in terror, our naughty father cut the main electric switch downstairs in the cellar and plunged the occupants of the drawing room into utter darkness. They must have thought it was the coming of Armageddon. Chaos as Mr Rainey called, 'Charlie' (our father was an electrician) 'Can you do something?' and Father, after a pause, switched on the power again, to be rewarded by Mr Rainey with a glass of whisky!

There were no more tributes to St Celia that night. Mrs Oyler was silenced at last. A gentle soul, she had no idea of the 'suffering' she caused.

Times change and different tastes in music prevail today. I still believe that we are diminished by the fact that there are now no Mrs Oylers.

I can still hear the voice of Charles Rainey saying, 'Mabel, are you going to sing for us?'

CHAPTER 19

Stark Terror

One balmy July evening in 1952 I was walking along the seashore with my eighteen month-old son Philip. We were listening to the music of the waves and the little fellow was fascinated by the feeling of them washing over his tiny feet. It was a superb evening at St Leonard's on Sea. As we strolled along the beach enjoying the secret, precious communion between father and son, we were blissfully happy, though each in his own way. With his tiny hand enclosed in mine we continued our walk, rejoicing in the sound of the waves and in the cool breeze enveloping us. All was serene.

Suddenly my boy was gone! He had slipped from my hand and fallen into a deep indentation in the beach which had been quite invisible up to that point. For moments of indescribable horror my little son was submerged and out of my sight, at the mercy of the merciless sea. Into the water I plunged, groping wildly for contact with him, but for interminable seconds I was unable to locate him. Unspeakable dread and panic gripped me as I floundered about, sick with pain and fear at the dreadful prospect of losing my little boy. Then by sheer chance a wave momentarily washed his submerged body towards me and it lightly brushed my leg. I seized his foot and dragged him ashore.

For some moments I lay clasping the little fellow to me and uttering a silent prayer of relief and thanksgiving. It had been a near thing. For the rest of that day I felt as though my innards had been scooped out.

Earlier I had undergone another terrible mishap with one of my children; this time it was my three year-old daughter, Nicolette. The year was 1949. We had crossed the busy road in Hayes, Middlesex, where we were then living, and were bound for the paper shop, where I was going to buy a newspaper and an ice-cream cornet for my little girl. As I put my hand in my pocket for money, I suddenly realised that she was no longer standing at my side. Instinct prompted me to race after her as she scampered off on flying little legs, heading for the exit. Tearing after her, I was just in time to pluck her from the bonnet of a passing lorry, which stopped with a screech of brakes. The driver was ashen-faced and so badly shaken that he had to be given a cup of tea before he could continue.

That day, when we so nearly lost our little daughter, she herself was blessedly oblivious of the sheer terror she had brought to her father. Today she is fifty-four, though looking thirty-four, and has two lovely boys.

When I recall these incidents, which I am sure many other parents could match, I realise that on occasion we are all moments away from death. Death leers with a mocking smile over the shoulders of every one of us. Let us, then, venerate the gift of each and every day and be gracious to our fellow men and women.

CHAPTER 20

Deutschland Über Alles

In 1961 the twelve-year-old son of a German colleague arrived at our home in Ealing, West London, to spend the summer holiday with our family and thus acquire the opportunity to improve his English and to learn something about our way of life.

He quickly formed a good rapport with our twelve-year-old son Philip, who swiftly introduced him to the mysteries of cricket, a game utterly foreign to young Manuel from Bielefeld. They kicked a ball around in nearby Cleveland Park, but cricket soon became the *cause célèbre* between them. Philip eagerly embraced the role of teacher, of initiator of our national game to the eager but somewhat bemused young German, who was puzzled by terms such as 'leg before wicket', a 'four' or a so-much-desired 'six' boundary and, of course, there was also the doom-laden word, 'OUT'!

The language difficulty made Philip's explanations rather protracted, but he demonstrated how to hold the bat and the correct stance before the wicket. Philip also tried to convey to the young German something of the sanctity of the wicket and how it should not be touched or its dignity in any way defiled. Manuel from Germany committed a heinous crime by fiddling with bails and was severely censured.

Drama and England's cricketing reputation were soon to be evoked when Philip instructed Manuel how to bowl. After several demonstrations, during which Philip explained that the ball must not be thrown, but should be delivered in a slow, or fast, circular action, Philip graciously agreed to bat first, for Manuel seemed most eager to bowl.

Now comes a moment of horror for England and for Philip. This German, on his very first appearance on the pitch . . . *bowled Philip out, spreadeagling the wicket with his first ball*!

My son was stupefied! Shock and disbelief suffused his countenance and I could see that something was going to happen. He threw his bat forty feet up in the air and, red-faced, he stalked off the field and headed for home. Manuel was greatly distressed. 'What have I made wrong?' he asked. I consoled him and much later that day I saw them together, jolly good friends again. Anglo-German relations were never quite the same, however, and there was no more talk about cricket.

Out shopping with my wife Peggy, Manuel spotted tins of Libby's condensed milk and said, 'Ach – German milch'. 'No Manuel, Libby's is an American company,' rejoined Peggy. A pause, then Manuel said emphatically: 'Then the cows are German.' How's that for patriotism?

CHAPTER 21

My Grandsons

Marcel

Our Marcel achieved first place in an intake of 150 for the Common Entrance Examination to the Twelfth-Century Public School of Merchant Taylors. Grandma and I celebrated the occasion with the following ode:-

> Let all salute his high endeavour,
> Laud his efforts, laud his play.
> Our Marcel did shrink – no never,
> From his duty on the day!
> They speak volumes, seven A grades,
> Of his energy and zest.
> Sustained study, dedication,
> Testify he is the BEST!
> So sing we all to our Marcel,
> A glorious Te Deum of praise,
> Go strong! Go High! Excel,
> And may God grant you golden days.

Pascal

Herewith Grandma and Grandpa's tribute to Pascal on the occasion of his stunning success in passing the Entrance Examination for the prestigious Christ's Hospital Public School. (An awful example of doggerel, for which I hope I shall be forgiven.)

> Those Porcherons show once again
> How well they play the Entry game.
> Young Pascal sat Christ's College Test,
> And proudly joins the very best
> Of this year's applicants.
> So now the Head of this great school,
> Quite contrary to the usual rule,
> In his own hand a postscript writes:
> Oh Pascal come and scale the heights
> Of academia's awesome peaks.

Our grandson Marcel in his last term at Merchant Taylors School.

Pascal, aged twelve at Christ's Hospital School, 1999.

Allow your grandpa to advise
A course to follow to be wise
Read every week one splendid book
Read William Blake and Rupert Brooke,
Immortal Shakespeare, Spenser, Pope,
Ah! Kipling too has much to say
To help a young man on his way.
So many other writers too, Pascal,
Await discovery by you.
Set sail for Elysium's golden shore,
There shall you find joy and more.
Avoid the shoals and hidden rocks,
And don't forget to change your socks!
In thought and deed be close to God.

Our daughter, Nicolette married a Frenchman, a Monsieur Claude Porcheron – hence the French Christian names of our grandsons, Marcel and Pascal.

PART II

The Royal Navy

I travelled among unknown men
In lands beyond the sea;
Nor, England, did I know till then
What love I bore to thee.

W. Wordsworth

The famous Shotley Mast, HMS Ganges. The author is 'button boy', right at the very summit.

CHAPTER 22

The Shotley Mast

HMS *Ganges* is the naval training establishment in East Anglia for Boy Sailors. It is famous throughout the world and its dominant feature is the Shotley Mast, vast and awe-inspiring, which the boys climb regularly as part of their training. It culminates at the very summit in a flat-topped 'button' and it is a special mark of distinction to be able to climb right up to the button and even to stand upright on it. For this part of our training my brother Billy and I were better prepared than most. Sons of the caretakers of a large house in Brixton, we had been accustomed to climbing the huge beech trees in the garden and with constant practice had developed the agility – and much of the fearlessness too – of monkeys. So familiar were we with the various handholds and footholds of those trees, that if I were to go back now, I should remember them as if it were yesterday.

Once arrived at HMS *Ganges*, I lost no time in meeting the challenge of the Shotley Mast and swiftly attained the button. On Saturdays I used often to be first up, and would settle down in that splendid vantage point to enjoy the thrilling vista reaching right over Harwich to Felixstowe. Nearer home, I had a wonderful view of the rugby matches and the flag-hoisting competitions going on below and would watch the bunting flying up and down. Up there I used to have a marvellous sense of freedom from authority. They could not get at me and I was monarch of all I surveyed. Most of all I used to enjoy that most illicit and strictly forbidden pleasure, a puff at a cigarette. To obtain cigarettes at all called for the utmost craft and ingenuity, and if you were caught in possession of them, you were severely caned. My mother sympathised and used to smuggle packets of Players' Virginia in to me hidden in dark-coloured jam. Up there on the button of the Shotley Mast, I could enjoy them to the full.

On my way up, I used to take special note of the final stage of the ascent, passing by the great wire hawsers supporting the mast and leading down to the ground. Just before reaching the button, you came to a part that was particularly smooth and polished. Often I felt an impulse to go down the wire itself, but again and again I resisted what seemed an act of sheer madness. Yet boys of sixteen fear nothing physical. One Saturday the

A British sailor in the line of Nelson, Drake, Jellico and Admiral Beatty – myself!

persistent impulse suddenly became irresistible and I yielded. Swinging my leg over the wire, I began my descent by that route. There could be no going back. Petrified though I was, I knew that I could not return to the Mast itself. I was short in stature and consequently in reach too; I had to go down the wire. I gripped it and began. Slowly I eased my way down, sick with fear but so absorbed in survival that I did not notice the pain in my hands or the blood on them until I reached the net. At the moment when I knew I had got away with it, a mighty surge of triumph – no, exultation! – swept over me. I had done it; I had come down the wire! No other lad, I believe, has since been foolish enough to attempt such a feat.

Did I say 'Got away with it'? Oh no! Waiting for me was the Officer of the Day and an RPO.[1] 'What do you think this is – a circus?' demanded the OOD. 'Commander's Report', he added. I got ten days' Number II's – and well deserved!

This was followed by another episode. One day, sitting on the button and king of the world, I wondered what it would be like to stand on my head right on the button itself. Coming up dead centre of the button was a strong weathervane. Gripping this with one hand, I placed my head, still in its cap, on the flat top of the button. Then, holding tight with the other hand to its side, I slowly raised my legs into the air. For a couple of moments I had an unusual upside-down view of the quarterdeck and parade. Not many knew about the insanity described above. Even fewer can even begin to imagine the thrill of it – unforgettable and indescribable. It did, however, receive a mention in the Press. William Hickey, the well-known journalist of the *Daily Express*, recorded the feat in his column.

---

1. An RPO is a Regulating Petty Officer. OOD equals Officer of the Day.

CHAPTER 23

Boxing Clever!

Boxing was a compulsory part of P.E. training at HMS *Ganges*. Thus it was that I found myself in the ring facing a short, stockily built boy named Alfie Coghlan, who came from a Yorkshire mining village.

Like so many gifted exponents of the ill-named 'noble art', outside the ring Alfie was a gentle, friendly boy, so that one was never aware of the deadly potential of his fists.

The rule was that each of us fifteen or sixteen year-olds had to box three two-minute rounds and how I longed to hear the bell that terminated hostilities at the end of each two-minute stretch – that is something no one will ever know.

In the ring, Alfie was a *fiend* – at once a remorseless punishment machine and a tantalising, unhittable target. One second he would be facing me. I would despatch a well-aimed left hook, only to punch the air. By the time it should have made contact, Alfie would be dancing away to my left or right as lightning quick and as superbly balanced as Rudolph Nureyev on the stage at Covent Garden. So quick and elusive was he that I doubt whether I landed a single punch. All this time his fists would be coming at me like twin rapid-firing anti-aircraft guns. My head would rock madly on my shoulders as I received those double blows, those awful, remorseless fusillades from Alfie, which made me see stars and lightning. A merciful bell signalled the end of round two and I turned to the P.E. Petty Officer in charge. 'That's it, Chief,' I said, 'I'm not going back into the ring for round three!'. 'You are yellow,' said the PO, 'You are a coward!' 'That's right,' I replied, 'I am'.

That PO got his revenge, for in a future and less punitive bout he announced, 'And in the *yellow* corner, Signal Boy Bell!' My young shipmates thoroughly enjoyed my discomfiture except for Alfie. 'Sorry if I hurt you, Ron,' he said. An extremely likeable young man. I hope that today he is a happy old grandfather like me, surrounded by family and friends in that Yorkshire village of his.

CHAPTER 24

The Admiral and Jimmy

The picture I see now in my mind's eye is the big parade ground of the RN barracks of HMS *Drake* in Devonport. It is the Monarch's birthday and approximately 800 men are dressed in their 'number ones' (best uniforms) ready for inspection by Admiral Sir Reginald Tyrwhitt, a portly figure looking slightly like a character in a comic opera with his cocked hat and sword.

In World War I he had had a highly distinguished career, in particular commanding the famous flotilla based on Harwich, whose regular sweeps of the North Sea kept it largely free of German forces. In this connection, one engagement is particularly worthy of mention. In April 1916 the Fifth Light Cruiser Squadron and accompanying destroyers encountered a powerful and vastly superior force of three German battle cruisers under the command of Rear Admiral Boedicker. Commodore Tyrwhitt, as he was then, was flying his flag in HMS *Conquest*. They were too late to prevent an attack on Lowestoft, where many houses were destroyed, but the Commodore was able to divert the enemy force from a planned bombardment of Great Yarmouth before obeying the traditional Naval tactic of retreating before a superior force. Thereby he and his gallant seamen certainly saved the popular seaside resort from a very nasty ordeal.

Later he became Admiral Sir Reginald Tyrwhitt, C. in C. The Nore. On the occasion I am speaking of, then, accompanied by his Flag Lieutenant and also by that most formidable of lower-deck personalities, the Master of Arms, he was moving down the line of stony-faced matelots (I know now what they were thinking!) when he came to the man standing next to me, a powerfully built rating from Lancaster, my shipmate, Jimmy Bradford. The ensuing dialogue went somewhat as follows:

The Admiral to Jimmy: 'How do you like life in the service?'

Jimmy (pausing for a moment): 'Well, it's all right for the likes of you, Sir!'

I was inches away from the Master of Arms (All such deities are called 'The Jaunty'). I saw a faint smile on the weather-beaten face of the Admiral, but the Master of Arms' face changed from pink to purple and

My shipmate, Jimmy Bradford, a lifelong friend. We had been boys together on HMS Ganges and it was he who was 'cheeky' to Admiral Tyrwhitt – and got away with it!

back to pink again. How glad we all were when the Admiral and entourage departed to the officers' mess for refreshment.

As for Jimmy, to everyone's relief and surprise, there were no repercussions for his 'insolence', but he never did forget the black menace of the look the Jaunty gave him after the parade.

CHAPTER 25

The Admiral's Boots

The Cruiser HMS *Leander*, flying the flag of Sir Percy Noble, is rolling and pitching in a rather rough North Atlantic sea. Her company, including even the experienced hands, are in some discomfort and most feel 'queasy'. No one thinks of food or even drink. A mood of dogged resignation prevails. It is 2100 hours, the time when Naval tradition ordains that the Officer of the Day and the Master at Arms inspect the ship from bow to stern and on each deck to ensure everything is properly secured and clean. On this particular night the Admiral, dressed for Dinner beneath his oilskins, decides to accompany the Officer of the Day on his 'rounds'. Now comes a moment of disaster for Signalman Bell!

My hammock was slung beside a steel ladder joining two decks. Just as the Admiral descended and his highly polished sea boots were level with my hammock, *Leander* gave a violent lurch to port and my unhappy stomach deposited my supper all over the Admiral's boots!

Deus misereatur! 'God be merciful!' I expected the majesty of the King's Rules and Admiralty Instructions, the Navy's legal code endorsed by Parliament, would be my fate and that I might, so to speak, be hung from the yard arm; but no disciplinary action followed. An indignant Petty Officer, muttering about, 'I don't know what the Navy is coming to', ordered me to 'turn out' of my hammock and 'get a bucket to mop up!'

The next morning the Admiral's batman, a large Royal Marine, gave me the sort of look that I imagine the boxer Tyson might give to anyone who crossed his bows. He had had to clean the Admiral's boots!

Admiral Noble, later Commander in Chief North Atlantic and then our wartime Naval Attaché in Washington, was the classical English aristocrat; he always looked immaculate and had that quiet air of authority so typical of the Royal Navy in its historical prime, when the Senior Service sustained the *Pax Britannica* from Trafalgar right up to the end of World War II.

CHAPTER 26

The King and I . . .

It took some sixty years for me to learn that I was the butt of a Royal joke. Via *Navy News*, I resumed acquaintance with former shipmate John Cannon, who was personal messenger to Captain Maikig Jones of the carrier HMS *Courageous*. In a recent letter John told me what his Majesty King George VI said as he bade farewell to the Captain on leaving the ship during the great Fleet Review of the 1930's.

I had the middle watch (midnight until 0400 hours) the night before the royal visit. It was customary for duty middle-watchmen from the signal staff to get their heads down (sleep) in a flag locker situated in a recess hidden behind the SDO (Signal Distributing Office), rather than make the long trek to the Mess and one's hammock.

Lost in the arms of Morpheus, I slumbered the sleep of the Good and the Just until suddenly awakened by a hubbub and the sound of many voices. I opened my eyes and beheld HM The King, the Captain and various VIP's from the Admiralty and very senior officers. The august assembly were peering down on me as I lay in my boudoir couch of large soft flags and pennants. I was petrified. I was in the wrong place at the wrong time! Our worthy Chief Yeoman saved me from dire disciplinary consequences by calling out, 'He's a middle-watchman, Sir'.

The Royal party moved away. 'This is it!,' I thought, 'I could lose my badge for good conduct!' but . . . no action was taken against me.

This affair was witnessed at close hand by the Captain's messenger, John Cannon, standing just a few feet away from HM The King. In a letter written some sixty years later, he told how he heard the King say to our Captain, as he stepped onto the gangway leading to the waiting Royal Barge, 'Oh, you'd better keelhaul that flagwagger!' (Flagwagger equals a signalman).

John Cannon, I must tell you, now lives in happy retirement in Paignton, Devon. He survived not only the sinking of HMS *Courageous*, but also the sinking of the County Class Cruiser, HMS *Dorsetshire*. A double survivor! As for me, I was on shore that terrible day when U29 sank the *Courageous*, taking with her to the seabed some 400 of my young shipmates.

I have, since the War, stood by the Naval War Memorial in Plymouth. I

This signalman is 'talking' via mechanical semaphore to the famous battleship, HMS Renown.

read down the long column of names, most not known to me . . . then I recognise a name and I see a shipmate I knew and joked with; then I see the place where, but for God's mercy, my name would have been. What a lottery is this life!

Note: Keelhauling was used long ago as a Naval punishment for very serious crimes at sea. It involved tying a man to a hawser or rope, putting him over the side and hauling him right under the ship's keel and up again on the ship's other side. A terrible ordeal, for the victim's lungs often burst and he would drown.

CHAPTER 27

Fleet Manoeuvres

Old hands who served during the 1930's will remember the Combined Fleet Manoeuvres, which were the major Naval exercises carried out each spring. Two great fleets set out from Home and Mediterranean ports to 'seek, find and engage the enemy', using the vast Atlantic as their playground. In those days the two battle fleets, with their escorting cruisers and destroyer flotillas, performed their task under full war conditions. Total radio silence, guns crews closed up at night, sleeping by the guns and deadlights down, we steamed without lights. I remember vividly one very exciting night in mid-Atlantic somewhere off the Azores. The time was around 0200 hours and we were *Leander*, flagship of the 2nd Cruiser Squadron, flying the flag of Admiral Sir Percy Noble. We knew that the mighty *Queen Elizabeth*, flagship of the Mediterranean Fleet, was somewhere close. Our Captain, Ross Turner, a real old sea dog who, it was claimed by the ship's company, never smiled, was determined to gain great honours for *Leander* and her company by surprising the battleship. The Captain spent literally hours on the bridge, leaving it only rarely in compliance with the demands of nature. He sat on his high stool and everyone on the bridge was tense and excited at the prospect of a triumphant 'attack' on the Med. Flagship. Somewhere out there in the darkness the famous battleship was steaming, and no doubt equally aware of our presence. Who would surprise whom?

That question was answered by a sudden and electrifying burst of star shell, which lit us up and revealed our presence in a few seconds of artificial daylight. Soon came the signal from HMS *Queen Elizabeth* . . . 'I consider to have sunk you'. Our Captain's face went grey with disappointment and, frowning with barely concealed anger, he strode off the bridge without a word. Our ship's company, however, regarded our dismissal from the exercise as a piece of very good luck! For us it meant that ship's lights could switch on and deadlights could be opened. No more eye-straining through the Atlantic mists and, most pleasant of all, we were headed for Barbados and some splendid shore leave. Incidentally, the Fleet wireless officer in the *Queen Elizabeth*, Flagship of the Mediterranean Fleet, was Lt. Commander Lord Louis Mountbatten. The Home Fleet Flagship was HMS *Nelson*. Great days!

CHAPTER 28

The Loss of HMS *Prince of Wales*

Sometimes I go 'to sea' again via my naval videos. Compiled with full Admiralty blessing by a wily old matelot from tapes lying around in the Imperial War Museum, in them I can see again the historic meeting aboard the USS *Augusta* between Sir Winston Churchill and President Roosevelt and the combined morning service on board the battle cruiser HMS *Prince of Wales*. Rations on British ships were short in those days, and it was a warming sight to see U.S. sailors each with a personal food parcel for a RN rating. How terrible to remember that the *Prince of Wales* was soon afterwards to be lost off Singapore with awful loss of life. It was massive folly on someone's part to expose this ship and her sister to Japanese air attack without air cover. I knew these beautiful, proud and graceful ships and have been 'in company' with them. On the return from America, the *Prince of Wales* passed through a North Atlantic convoy and as she steamed through the lines of merchantmen to noisy greetings from ships' sirens, many semaphore messages of greeting were exchanged. Somehow everyone felt the presence of Sir Winston Churchill and was elated by it.

Later a storm! I clasp the side of our settee and hold on. I recall similar storms in the North Atlantic and in the Bay of Biscay that live with me still.

A severe Atlantic storm, with the quarterdeck of the cruiser,
HMS Leander *awash, 1935.*

CHAPTER 29

Sunday Divisions

Sunday, and, in accordance with ancient tradition, all hands, clad in their number one's (best suits), assembled on the quarterdeck for Divine Service.

I was spared that day for I was on duty watch on the flag deck. I had a splendid view, however, of the service in progress aboard HMS *Ceres*. The chaplain, or 'sin bosun', as he was usually called, perched precariously on a capstan with his surplice flowing wildly. He was probably telling his reluctant and captive congregation about the mystery of the Holy Trinity (It was Trinity Sunday). He may not have suspected that these men would rather be below decks playing cards, writing letters home, making tea or indulging in idle jests and banter. He announced the hymn, which drifted across to us in *Calypso* sounding like this:

> Crarn 'im wiv many crarns
> The Lamb upon his frone
> 'Ark ow the 'eavenly angels sing
> Crarn 'im Lord of all
> Crarn 'im, crarn 'im, crarn 'im Lord Gawd almighty
> Gawd in free persons, blessed Trinity

It was hardly of the vocal quality of a Welsh male voice choir, but the tones of these modern stentors would not have disgraced the heralds of the Trojan Wars.

On our bridge we all listened to those naval choristers with a feeling that all must be well with the world. Our young public school Lieutenant Officer of the Watch smiled broadly. 'She's a Chatham ship!' he said.

CHAPTER 30

A Nod and a Wink. An Odd Train Journey

In the '30's and '40's sailors from the London region whose Port Division was Devonport used to catch the 0140 express from Paddington, arriving in Plymouth North Road about 0630, just in time for breakfast in 'Aggie Weston's'.

In those days the train was full of Navy men and everyone tried to secure a corner seat, which gave some hope of a sleep. On this particular train I found myself in the centre seat, but I noticed in a corner seat on the other side a smartly dressed lady engrossed in a book and apparently oblivious to her Naval travelling companions.

In the opposite corner seat was a sailor unknown to me, who thus found himself opposite the elegant female. The train moved off and as everyone was English, nobody spoke until we were well past Reading, but even then little was said and we resigned ourselves to a quiet journey as the train hurtled westward.

It was then that I noticed some rather odd behaviour on the part of the sailor sitting opposite the lady. He kept trying to hide his face with a newspaper and shifting about in his seat.

Did he, I wondered, have piles or St Vitus's dance? The fidgeting continued and fellow passengers began to give him disapproving looks. By now he was blushing and struggling to suppress inner and uncontrollable mirth – what was his problem?

I studied the lady opposite him and at last realised the source of that sailor's embarrassment. The lady had an optical impediment which caused her, every minute or so, to give a pronounced wink.

The situation was close to boiling point and the sailor rose, desperate to avoid hurting the lady's feelings and, with his face covered with a handkerchief, he stumbled out into the corridor. I waited a while and then left to join my unknown shipmate. I found him in a state of near collapse. 'At first,' he said, 'I thought she was after me, but it took me a while to realise that she was not winking at me at all.'

We went to the restaurant car and stayed there a long time. On our return to our seats, the lady had dozed off and the sailor followed suit. She got out at Taunton and our journey ended without further disturbance.

When I said farewell to that sailor, I said: 'You have been Taunted!' I never saw him again.

CHAPTER 31

My Devonport Redhead

I first saw her through the steam of the fish and chip shop just outside the dockyard gates. A lovely redhead, with that Devonshire complexion compared often with that county's famous cream. I made a date and the following Sunday found myself on the Hoe, sitting on the grass beside this glorious creature. My cockney ears had a problem with her rich rolling Devonian accent, but together we watched the sun go down and listened to the murmuring of the city of Plymouth; we listened to the low hum of many thousands of voices and saw the sea of colour across the famous Sound. We sat together and I imbibed her fragrance. I saw my redhead several times and once thought *'this must be it'*, but the exigencies of the Service interrupted our romance and when I returned to Plymouth, I saw her again on the Hoe – but this time in the company of a well-built stoker! Betrayed!

Shortly after this, I had another affair of the heart; this time she was a young lady from Bideford in Devon, who was a domestic in Plymouth. It was a very short-lived affair, for I met her in a dance hall and took half the evening to pluck up courage to ask for a dance (I can't dance!) I swayed and tottered around the floor with yet another peaches-and-cream Devonian and thought things were going rather well until I asked her if I might escort her home.

'What do you think I am,' she demanded scornfully, 'a kidnapper?' Exit Ronald, who returned to HMS *Drake* on all fours! (She was somewhat older).

CHAPTER 32

'Rosie' Barlow

The Royal Naval Barracks in Devonport, known as HMS *Drake*, was, and still is today, a temporary home for sailors awaiting draft to HM ships.

For these men there are large recreation rooms, where off-duty sailors can relax, spin a yarn with shipmates, listen to the radio, write letters home, or simply sit and doze in comfortable armchairs. One day I found myself seated next to a young Able Seaman known as 'Rosie' Barlow, because of his high complexion. 'Would you like to see some photographs?' he said. Realising that I had to say yes or be discourteous, I agreed and accepted the fact that I was in for a boring few minutes looking at someone else's family. 'Rosie' showed me pictures of his parents and other family members and I made the appropriate admiring noises. Suddenly he showed me a photograph of a gloriously beautiful young lady. My heart stopped! A goddess with a face inexpressibly pure and lovely, like Michael Angelo's Madonna. She had a figure that would have turned Venus de Milo green with envy. 'That's Jean, my sister,' said A/B Barlow, 'Would you like a date?' What a question! I wondered how he could be so certain she would agree to meet me. 'Don't worry about that,' said 'Rosie', 'She will be there,' 'When,' he continued, 'are you next watch ashore?' 'Thursday,' I said. 'Right,' said A/B Barlow, 'Be outside the Military public house at 1900 hours and she will be there'.

It was only Tuesday and the long wait until Thursday drained my reserves of patience to their limits. At last Thursday came and I glided through the barrack gates on a cloud of joyous expectation. From 1900 hours I would be in a sailor's Elysium – close to a goddess.

It was a wet November evening when I arrived at the Military tavern. I felt like that German soldier meeting Lili Marlene underneath a lamppost. Sure enough, there was a female figure enveloped in a raincoat with her head obscured by a hood. 'Are you Ronald?' she enquired in a sweet soft voice. 'Yes' said I and then I suffered a terrible shock, peeping eagerly into the hood to see my Madonna's face. It was another young lady – with glasses and protruding teeth! I had lead in my heart and in my boots. 'Jean couldn't come,' Sadie explained, for that was her name. Overcoming my disappointment, I said, 'Shall we go to the pictures?' 'Yes,' said Sadie. I bought 2/3d tickets (a grievous blow to my naval finances) and we sat in rear seats. Sadie proved a very sweet and delightful companion and her quality purged my mean heart of its earlier disappointment. She rested her head (she had very nice hair) on my shoulder and she gave me one sweet soft kiss that sent me back to barracks very contented. 'Shall I see you again?' asked Sadie. 'Oh Sadie, I'm going to sea next Monday, but perhaps when I get back to Devonport.' I never saw her again and I do hope she found a good man to share her life.

Next day I saw 'Rosie' again. 'You rat,' I said. A/B Barlow, who must have been a very mischievous schoolboy, grinned and said, 'Ron, my boy, you'd better forget my sister. She's engaged to a Petty Officer Stoker.' But I shall remember Sadie.

CHAPTER 33

Louisa Ingleski

On a courtesy visit to North German ports in July 1934, HMS *Leander* was secured alongside the jetty in the then German city of Stettin, on the river Oder.

It was a balmy day, with bright sunshine and a steady stream of civilians walked up the gangway to enjoy a visit to this fine ship, flying the flag of Admiral Sir Percy Noble.

Off watch and fancy-free, I watched the visitors come aboard and soon two female figures stepped onto the steel deck with hesitant uncertain steps. It was a mother and daughter. My heart jumped and missed a couple of beats for the young lady was entrancingly beautiful, with shoulder-length golden hair and a lovely face and figure. I stepped forward to offer my services as a guide and, though they had little English and I no German, we managed to communicate satisfactorily.

I took them on the foc'sle and showed them the anchor and huge anchor cable lying like a gigantic watch chain. We then inspected A and B turrets before ascending the steel ladder leading to the flag deck and compass platform.

I took special pleasure in showing them where I worked on the flag deck, with its scrubbed deck, flag lockers and semaphores, mechanically worked by hand, and also our signal lamps and yard arm and masthead flashing lights. I could see they were getting a bit weary so I took them below decks to my mess deck, where I served them with hot tea and ship's biscuits.

It was time for visitors to leave and I escorted them to the gangway. 'I shall never see that heavenly girl again', I thought and my being began to flood with misery. We had exchanged smiles; she had a sweet radiant smile with lovely eyes of deepest blue.

Just as I was about to take my leave, her mother, after a quick exchange with her daughter in German, said: 'You kom to our house?' She took an envelope from her purse and wrote: 'Ingleski, Drewshof VIII'. I made them understand that I could visit them on Thursday and wrote the date. I also put the time, 1300 hours. Louisa, for that was my goddess's name, pointed to a building opposite the gangway and indicated that she would be there to meet me.

She was there and took me home to meet the family. I had a meal with them, but although my conversation was limited, on the whole they understood my explanations about my family in London.

Louisa indicated that we should go for a walk and, as the evening slowly banished the happy day, she took me to the beautiful Quistor Park, a green idyllic place with flowers everywhere and plenty of quiet recesses where the romantically involved could pass time together.

In this park I knew I loved her. Afraid for so long to touch or try to hold her in my arms, she seemed to sense my shyness for she touched my hand tenderly. Thus encouraged, I put my arm around her shoulders and snuggled up to her. We just sat there and allowed an hour or so to pass without the need to say a word. The trees danced gently in a slight breeze and as the sun disappeared, we languished in a dream of love and utter bliss.

During the next three days the ship was in Stettin, Louisa took me around the city, but the hour arrived when we were to leave and proceed down river for Cuxhaven, the Kiel Canal and Plymouth, our home port. I managed to get ashore a couple of hours before we sailed and there she was, my beautiful Louisa. I learned that day the pain of parting. She whispered, 'Ich liebe dich' and, for the first and only time, I kissed her. Her lips were warm and moist and it seemed an eternity before I let her go. Time was running out fast and I just reached the gangway in time before it was hoisted and stowed on board.

As *Leander* moved slowly down river, I, on the flag deck, could see her holding a white handkerchief. As we gathered way, she ran alongside the jetty holding her handkerchief above her head. I could not wave or respond, for such behaviour is not tolerated on British warships on official visits. A German Army band played our national anthem and our Royal Marine band on the quarter deck responded with 'Deutschland über Alles'.

Louisa and I wrote regularly about once a month from August 1934 until December 1938, when, enclosed with a letter from my mother, was a letter, not in Louisa's handwriting, instructing me not to write again as Louisa was to marry someone else. I complied, for at a time when the Nazi frenzy was approaching its climax, I might have got her into difficulty with the Party.

I worked hard at the German language, inspired by Louisa. I gained an 'A' Level from the Royal Society of Arts and found the language very helpful during my frequent visits to Germany after I had left the Navy.

And then one day, thinking about Louisa and wondering if she was safe and happy, I came to realise that my Louisa was a reincarnation of Lore, the legendary Rhine maiden whose beauty drove rejected suitors to enter a monastery or take their lives.

She inspired that famous German song with the immortal words by Heinrich Heine. This legend is the quintessence of German romanticism Louisa too had golden hair and like Lore, her beauty and grace were enough to flood the heart with longing. According to legend, Lore aroused jealousy from her contemporary women, who, together with rejected suitors, accused her of being in touch with the devil and Lore was duly taken before the Archbishop of Cologne who held his court in Coblenz. Confronted with this girl who radiated virtue and purity, the Archbishop refused to bow to the wishes of her enemies and ordained that she should retire to a convent to await the return from the Crusades of her true love, the brave knight Frederick von Fürstenburg. If he did not return, she must take vows and give her life to God.

On her journey to the convent, situated on an island in mid-river where the Rhine joins the Moselle, Lore obtained the consent of her escorts to climb, for the last time, to look at the vineyards, castles and hills of the beautiful region before retreating from the world. She ascended the great rock of St Goar and saw a boat in the distance showing the colours of her lover, the Knight Frederick. Overcome with joy, she stood to wave a greeting, lost her foothold and plunged into the swirling waters of the river she loved.

Some say that men of faith and pure hearts are able to understand the mythical character of the Rhine region. Such men can muse by the rock of St Goar and see the Rhine maiden combing her golden hair and looking as she has done for almost a thousand years for her valiant knight, Frederick von Fürstenburg.

Her song and the plaintive sound of her harp still have the power to lure men to their doom. It is an enigma that virtue and beauty often end in tragedy – but is not that a frequent experience in all our lives?

Yes, Louisa was my Lorelei. Is it just possible that in the now-Polish city of Szczecin (Stettin), a once very beautiful old lady sits in her chair, thinking sometimes of her Naval Knight – Ronald Bell, ex-Signalman, Royal Navy?

Her last letter was very affectionate and it had long been understood that she would come to Britain and become my wife. Fate stole my Louisa but sent in her place my lovely English rose, my wife of almost sixty years.

Herewith the opening lines of the Lorelei by Heinrich Heine:

> I do not know the meaning of my sadness
> It stems from an old legend which will not leave me

Above, a very free translation; far better ones you can read in your local library. I am greatly indebted to Herr Arthur Kusche and his English translator Ms. Elsie Palmer for the Lorelei story. Their delightful book is entitled *Legends of the Rhine*.

CHAPTER 34

The Singapore General Hospital, 1936

At one time, while on board the base ship HMS *Terror* in Singapore, I found myself suffering from a severe bout of what the Germans call *Verstopfung*. Day after day passed, and I still could not achieve that daily act of deliverance essential to health. Among my shipmates, my condition aroused both interest and concern and on appearing in the Mess each morning, I would be greeted with: 'Any luck today, Ron?' Indeed, animated discussions used to be carried on as my sympathetic shipmates sought a solution to my problem. Secretly, I believe, they were enjoying my daily embarrassment.

Many and varied were the suggestions of these messmates of mine for solving the problem. Some of their remedies were drastic indeed and quite unprintable. The most alarming, I suppose, was that I should be depth-charged!

The ship's doctor, a Surgeon Lt. Commander, plied me daily with doses of that dreadful Navy remedy for all ailments, the vile-tasting 'white mixture'. Ugh! When even this proved of no avail, he said: 'Bell, I am sending you to hospital.'

Thus it was that I found myself in a nice clean bed, complete with Persil-white sheets and pillow, next to a German merchant seaman. What disorder he was suffering from I never discovered, but whatever it was, he was not allowed solid food. The hospital food was far better than that served by our ships' cooks, and that German suffered torture as he watched me dive into the tasty meals provided for me. In the end, unable to control my compassion, I used to pass him food when the nurses were looking the other way and he would devour it in total disregard of his condition. The beds had been placed sufficiently close for us to talk in fractured English, and he taught me a German card game called 'Sixty-Six'. He was a very pleasant young man of about my own age, and he hailed from Hamburg, a city I was to visit often in later years.

A terrible moment came when a small, pretty and very masterful Chinese nurse said: 'You are going to have an enema'. Placing a screen round me, she produced the fearsome instrument appropriate to my condition. Once I realised that this little lady was intending to administer

HMS Terror, *Singapore Base Ship.*

the cure herself, I made a vigorous protest. 'Let me do it, please,' I begged. 'Lie on your side and be quiet!' responded this adorable little tyrant. I can report that the treatment was a *roaring* success!

I blew a month's pay taking this charming Chinese maiden to dinner. She was a truly wonderful little lady, whose friendship I valued greatly for the rest of my time in Singapore. She was eager to learn all she could about Britain, especially England and London, and I was able to show her numerous photographs.

In my ward in the Singapore General Hospital the patients were mainly Chinese, with a sprinkling of Malays and Europeans. In the far corner of our ward was a very old and wizened Chinaman. His face was waxen and emaciated. His family – about thirty of them – used to visit him daily and crowd around his bed. Tiny children, adults and several matrons fussed over the poor old chap and he must have been much loved. The Chinese are very family-orientated and revere their old people much more than we do in the West.

One night I awoke about 0200 hours. The ward was silent except for snores. As I looked at the old man in the corner, a shiver went down my spine. In Singapore the moonlight is very strong and the moon is like a torch held in the hand of God. It covers everything in a white light and it encircled the ashen face of that old man, revealing it as a ghoulish mask. That night he died.

I have to award full marks to that hospital and to the high professional standard prevailing there. That nurse and the old Chinese gentleman live on in my memory.

CHAPTER 35

HMS *Calypso*, Immingham

The old C class light cruiser, a relic of World War I, was swinging round a buoy off Immingham, Hull, a couple of cables away from her sister, HMS *Ceres*.

The Leading Seaman in charge of our mess was a lean six-footer from London, who was responsible for our behaviour and well-being. There were seven in our mess. This leading hand was an ex-grammar school boy and therefore better educated than his charges. He treated us with a faint disdain and regarded himself as a superior person. We lesser mortals did not enjoy being the object of his sarcasm and ill-disguised contempt.

Our ship was a canteen messing ship, which meant that our daily menu was decided by the leading hand. This was different from the system in big ships, where every mess shared, or suffered (!) the same menu.

'Lofty', as our leading hand was known, fancied himself as a cook of the mess. The food was cooked in the galley but prepared for our mess by 'Lofty', who was responsible for spending each man's daily victualling allowance wisely and for ensuring that we were nourished sufficiently well to carry out our duties.

This man took his culinary duties very seriously. It gave us an opportunity to take our revenge for his irritating airs and graces. Here is how we secured that sweet revenge.

One day, in a manner similar to that of the Head Chef in the Dorchester Hotel, he announced: 'Tonight I have a special treat for you – but you must wait until I serve it as I want to surprise you.' We feigned eager anticipation. We saw him with a large pan, mixing milk, cheese and margarine, but had no idea what was in store. Time at last for our evening meal. Out of a big pan he served portions of what looked a gooey mess, saying: 'Spread it on your bread'. 'What is it?' someone asked. 'Welsh Rarebit,' replied 'Lofty', looking somewhat pained.

In fact this dish, unfamiliar to some of us, tasted very nice, but we were careful not to show any enthusiasm. Silently we finished the meal without laudatory comment.

As we turned in and climbed into our hammocks, our plan came into operation. 'Lofty' was sitting up straight in his hammock and reading one of the classics as usual. Then from a corner of the mess came a loud groan. 'What's the matter, shipmate?' said a voice. 'I've got a pain in my stomach,' replied the 'sufferer'. 'Pipe down and it will go,' he was advised. Some minutes later a loud cry again broke the silence. 'I've got bloody awful bellyache,' said a voice from another hammock. 'You'd better see the quack in the morning,' said another voice. Again some minutes quiet before yet another cry of 'pain': 'It must be something we've eaten,' said a mischievous voice.

Our leading hand, red-faced and angry, said: 'You miserable b'stds, you're not used to decent food. You deserve to starve.'

Loud laughter from all hands and we all settled down for a good sleep in rather better humour than usual. Perhaps I imagined it, but 'Lofty' seemed to be a little nicer towards us after our 'Welsh Rarebit' feast.

CHAPTER 36

The Three-Legged Elephant

Sailors are notorious storytellers. It may be the long periods of isolation at sea away from normal human contacts that forces them to imagine events which perhaps never happened. Thus 'spinning a yarn' is a frequent pastime aboard ships as a counter to boredom.

Some sailors' yarns are a great strain on our credulity. A sailor I met in the China Fleet Club back in the '30's in Hong Kong was one whom I declined to believe and I was convinced he was 'pulling my leg'. Here is his story.

About a couple of hundred miles from Bombay, where he had been sent to convalesce, he was taken to a small local zoo where, in his words, 'I saw the only three-legged elephant in the world.' I said, 'Nonsense, no such animal could survive because it would be completely immobile, unable to walk. Pull the other one.'

'Will you believe your own eyes?' he asked and took out of his jumper an envelope with a photograph of an elephant apparently with only three legs. I examined the photo under a borrowed magnifying glass and could see neither a fourth leg nor any sign of abnormality. The animal's skin seemed smooth and bore no evidence at all of any missing limb.

Still unconvinced but puzzled by the photograph, I asked: 'Did you see the elephant in motion?' 'Yes,' said this sea-borne zoologist, 'He had a kind of shuffling gait, using his single leg as a kind of balance rather like a tiller, and he had a permanent list to port! He moved along quite well,' concluded the sailor.

Suddenly he leaned forward and said: 'Look here, mate, my funds are low and I need some cash. I will sell you this picture for twenty Hong Kong dollars. It might one day be valuable.'

I gave him fifteen – all I had, and he took it with a smile and said, 'One day you'll be glad you bought that photograph.'

Now, dear readers, study this photograph closely and answer the question: was I, in modern parlance, conned? I bet you will not find that fourth leg!

The Three-legged Elephant.

CHAPTER 37

Petty Officer J. Fisher

In today's paper I read that soldiers are to be given the legal right to sue their COs!

Good God! This is political correctness gone raving mad! Truly Britain is an asylum. What effect will this have on army discipline?

I reflect ruefully. What a pity we ratings aboard HMS *Leander* did not have such legal power to protect ourselves against a certain long-gone Petty Officer who terrorised us young ratings on that cruiser's flag deck for some two and half years. He was a prototype Hitler! Drunk with power as the one responsible for the immaculate cleanliness of that Flagship's flag deck, he hounded us all with cold indifference to our protests. Scrub and polish where everything was already pristine. My shipmates and I often discussed, half seriously, whether we should wait till dark and tip him over the side.

Voice pipes of brass were polished several times daily; the deck was scrubbed until you could have eaten your meals on it; all ropes and halyards were neatly coiled and the heads and tacks of flags and pennants were neatly stowed in the flag lockers.

On occasion, when we were dressed in our No. 1's for a run ashore, he would say, 'There is water in those gun bays. I want it cleaned up before you go ashore!' At such times, it is safe to say, our feelings toward him would certainly have led us to sue him had we that legal right.

Yet, when we were inspected by our Admiral or our Captain and they showed approval of all our efforts, we felt a gush of pride, and when such illustrious ones had departed and PO Fisher had a shadow of a smile for us, we felt a certain pride in our fine ship and even a passing approval of our tyrannical Petty Officer.

As we watched him go down the gangway for 14 days leave, we felt that he would receive his just deserts when in the company of Mrs F., back home in Bristol.

I'll not forget his rich Bristolian accent when summoning us for some unwelcome task. He would say, 'Come yerrr my luvvers'.

CHAPTER 38

RN Destroyers in Rough Weather

The two old World War I Destroyers accompanying HMS *Leander* in a severe North Atlantic storm were bucking like broncos in an angry sea.

One minute we could see their whirling screws before they vanished into a deep valley, then we saw their bows pointed heavenwards with water rushing off their fo'c's'les so that they appeared for a second or two like dogs shaking water after a swim.

As we watched them, Admiral Sir Percy Noble was likewise watching on *Leander's* bridge. He could see the wildly swinging masts silhouetted against a silver moon above a sullen sea, and was concerned that the violence of the storm might endanger the Destroyers' men. Accordingly he requested our Chief Yeoman of Signals to ask those tormented little ships to report their situation.

Back, via winking signal lamp, came the answer: 'Very comfortable, thank you!'

British understatement! The Admiral shook his head and smiled; he was, I suspect, a proud man.

CHAPTER 39

Midshipmen, Royal Navy

Carefully selected boys, mainly from famous public schools, enter the Royal Navy for training as future officers. Today there are but few, for in terms of manpower the Navy is much reduced, but in the Service in which I served, there were hundreds of them.

Midshipmen received the same basic training in seamanship, signals and other naval disciplines as Seamen Boys. My story is about one young midshipman, Midshipman Culme-Seymore, the son of an Admiral.

Almost the sole privilege of midshipmen was in the manner in which they were addressed. In marching, the Chief Petty Officer in charge would say, 'pick your feet up' or 'swing those arms, *Mr* Brown,' or whatever the name was.

As a Boy Seaman, the lowest form of life aboard a warship, it was my daily duty to lash up the hammock of Mr Culme-Seymour. This young man was a lazy fellow first thing in the morning, and very slow at turning out of his hammock. He had to wrench himself from the arms of Morpheus with the consequence for me that on return to the boys' mess, I would find those young 'wolves', my shipmates, had devoured most of the porridge or other breakfast food. A matter for real chagrin!

I told my Petty Officer of my deprivations and he decided to sidestep the normal, somewhat protracted, 'Complaints' procedure by marching me along to the Quarter Deck, where I was able to make my lamentations to the Officer of the Watch. This young Lieutenant, a true public school type, listened to my story and said, after a brief moment of reflection, 'Carry on Bell'. And that is all he said. Somewhat crestfallen, I thought that was an end to the matter.

Next morning Midshipman Culme-Seymore was already up and gone when I arrived in the midshipmen's flat to lash his hammock. And so it was every morning thereafter.

Later that same day I saw Midshipman Culme-Seymour and expected a frosty look. No – he grinned a friendly grin and I gave him a salute worthy of an Admiral. A very nice young man.

This story demonstrates that the old Royal Navy was a very humane and democratic service, despite its love of tradition and discipline.

Many years later, after I had left the Navy, I was heading for Oxford
Circus on the Central Line underground when, for some strange reason I
departed from my normal choice of newspaper and bought *The Times*
instead. I browsed through its (in those days) illustrious pages and came to
the obituary notices.

I could not believe what I saw: the obituary notice of Commander F.
Culme-Seymour, my midshipman of long ago.

I saw his pleasant cheeky face and that grin again. It was an emotional
moment.

CHAPTER 40

HMS *Superb*, Newcastle

My Naval brother, one of the Royal Navy's most decorated sailors in World War II (he has 11 medals), told me the following rollicking stories from his Navy days.

The Cruiser *Superb* lies off Newcastle and leave is granted to both watches, who eagerly set out to explore the city's taverns and imbibe the famous Newcastle Ale. My brother, Petty Officer Bell, and another PO spend a very happy evening in various taverns. So content are they that they forget their intention to return to the ship, and in any case are too late to catch the last liberty boat. They need to find beds for the night.

In a strange city and without contacts, they decide to ask a taxi driver where they can find lodgings for one night. 'I know a nice lady who will put you up,' says the cabby, 'hop in and I will take you – it's not far'. They duly arrive in a nice road with neat front gardens and attractively decorated exteriors. A well-kept suburban enclave with tree-lined pavements. The two Petty Officers think they are in for a certain degree of luxury when the cab stops outside number 84. They pay him, giving him a nice tip for his assistance.

They knock on the door, which soon opens to reveal a well-built, handsome lady who welcomes them inside and says: 'I expect you're hungry, so I'll get you boys something to eat'. She takes them upstairs to a clean but rather small bedroom, where they have a wash and brush-up before dinner. My brother Bill and his shipmate Joe feel that this is going to be a great run ashore and they enjoy a good meal. They are especially fascinated by the attentive landlady's rich 'Geordie' accent. Her late husband, she tells them, was a merchant seaman, 'so I'm used to sailors,' she says with a flirtatious smile. After the meal Billy explains that they will have to leave early because they are due back on board by 0800 hours. 'So, if you will excuse us,' says Bill, 'we'll turn in now and get some sleep'.

Two very heterosexual sailors climb into bed and prepare to spend a few hours in the arms of Morpheus. At this point there is a gentle knock on the door. None too pleased, Joe calls, 'come in', and in comes this voluptuous lady with two cups of Ovaltine. She is wearing a flowered dressing gown, beneath which, it transpires, she is naked! 'Drink up, boys,' says the lady,

My brother Billy. One of the Navy's most decorated sailors.

gradually shedding her dressing gown, to reveal that she is indeed very beautiful, with a breathtaking figure, a feature of which is two very generous breasts. Taken aback, my brother Bill says: 'Oh Madam, we are both married and we just want to get some rest.'

After a brief silence she explodes. 'You're a pair of nancy boys,' she shouts, growing ever more terrifying by the minute, 'Get out, you miserable b*****ds, Get Out!'

This is a time to remember one of the first principles of Naval warfare: Withdraw before a superior force! So the two Petty Officers dress hurriedly and make for the front door. Joe is outside first and whilst waiting for Billy to do up his laces, narrowly misses a soaking, for the outraged lady empties a bucket of water out of the top window. 'Let's get out of here,' says Billy, and both men run off into the Newcastle early hours, the air alight with the curses of a disappointed lady ringing in their ears.

HMS *Superb* left next morning, heading for the relative peace of Korean waters.

CHAPTER 41

'Arrest That Man!'

The second Billy Bell Naval story tells of the time, now long gone, when the mighty Home Fleet assembled at Invergordon in Scotland. The great battleships, cruisers and destroyers cast hundreds of thirsty sailors on the barren wastes of the famous old base. These men had scarcely any recreational facilities. They could kick a football, but most spent their time in the canteen or walking around the little Scottish town.

Alcohol affects some men in a way that transforms a normally amiable chap into an aggressive nuisance – a danger to himself and others. A crowd of men were waiting on the jetty for liberty boats to convey them back to their ships. One such liberty boat was under the charge of a fresh-faced midshipman, a mere schoolboy. This midshipman was soon to be tested! A very large, heavily built sailor, very much under the weather and very bellicose, shouted to the young midshipman: 'Does your mummy know you're out?' Who washes your nappies? Where's your pram?' and sundry other gross insults. At first the young officer decided to ignore this drunken sailor, but when his insults appeared to have no effect, the man became inflamed. He strode nearer to the midshipman, who now realised it was time to act. Turning to my brother Bill, who is of diminutive stature, he said: 'Petty Officer, arrest that man!'

Somewhat aghast, brother Billy, with all the magisterial authority of his senior lower deck rank, advanced towards the swaying giant of a man. 'I have to arrest you,' he said. 'You lay a finger on me and I'll put you on your back!' retorted the big fellow. 'Now come on, man,' said little Billy quietly, 'I need your help. If I don't take you in, I'll be in the rattle (trouble) too.' Make it easy on me and for yourself'. A few anxious moments later and the big fellow seemed to have discovered reserves of fraternal feeling for Billy. His bellicosity subsided as he accompanied PO Billy Bell to the liberty boat and incarceration in the ship's detention quarters.

At defaulters next day, now sober and contrite, and after brother Billy had put in a good word, the Commander said: 'You've been a bloody fool, A/B Foster, but your reports are good and there was no violence. However, your behaviour toward that midshipman was thoroughly reprehensible and I award you ten days stoppage of leave and pay. Dismiss'.

Billy and A/B Foster exchanged mutually complimentary smiles – a happy ending after all. The Navy is a very tolerant institution.

One ship in particular in which my brother served comes forcibly to mind – HMS *Warspite*. The following brief remarks, dedicated to the memory of those who served in her, might perhaps be considered not wholly irrelevant as a conclusion to this brief account of episodes in Billy's career. It concerns the part *Warspite* played in the Battle of Jutland as well as in the Second World War.

'At the Battle of Jutland HMS *Warspite* came under heavy fire from the German High Seas Fleet and suffered severe damage. In the course of the Second World War she defied the Luftwaffe and the combined naval forces of Germany and Italy.

'Is it not strange that this historic old warship refused the cruel indignity of the breaker's yard and en route to that yard, broke her towline and cast herself on the rocks in Cornish waters?

'Do ships have souls? I believe they do. The departed spirits of her gallant companies are distilled into a mysterious presence that pervades decks and bulwarks for ever. Her men never leave her.'

CHAPTER 42

Miss Agnes Weston Naval
(Sailors) Hostels in RN Ports

Agnes Weston was a lady of the early part of the last century whose name is enshrined in the hearts of all Royal Navy sailors, past and present.

In her time and for most of the last century, up to and including the end of World War II, the Navy was a global force whose presence on the great oceans guaranteed the peace for over a hundred years. The number of men needed to man the Home and Mediterranean Fleets, plus a powerful Naval presence in China, the East and West Indies, was enormous, so that on any one day or night the numbers of sailors on the streets of our Naval towns, Chatham, Portsmouth and Devonport, were quite enough to cause problems for police and civilians.

These young men, far from home and often very lonely, filled the taverns, cinemas and dance halls and caused many an anxious moment for parents with daughters.

Generally well behaved, their days on shore were empty and often led to drunkenness and disorder on the streets. Naval police had a busy time at weekends, yet, on the whole it can be said that local people approved of Jack Tar.

Ms. Weston felt genuine sympathy for these young sailors and she established hostels in each Naval town where ratings could get a clean bed and a decent meal for one shilling and sixpence. A strict evangelical, who saw alcohol as the main source of a sailor's downfall, in these hostels she stressed the virtue of temperance. When a man entered 'Aggie's' he was expected to sign a pledge to give up the demon drink and those who did not sign the pledge forms felt guilty.

'Aggie's' had two floors of cubicles with wafer-thin wooden partitions, so that one could hear the man in the next cubicle snore or scratch himself. Each cubicle had a clean bed, a chamber pot and a covering of wire netting. One felt rather like a chicken. On the wall a framed message bore the words 'Jesus Loves You'. Another notice in each cubicle read, 'Under no circumstances must more than one rating occupy this cubicle.'

Miss Weston would certainly have put the Royal Navy under the protection of Clause 28.

At 0600 in the morning sailors were roused from their slumber by a member of staff walking down the aisles ringing a very noisy bell, similar to one used in school playgrounds to summon pupils back to their classrooms.

The ensuing din led to a period when the air was purple with catcalls from awakened matelots. The bell-carrier was the most abused man in Devonport, or, indeed, in the entire great city of Plymouth.

Breakfast followed, consisting of fried bread, eggs, bacon and a large mug of hot tea. Restored to good humour, Jack reported back on board by 0900.

No sailor who enjoyed that mixture of evangelical fervour and a good bed and night's sleep can ever forget 'Aggie', or the temperance slogans on the walls reading:

'For sin and crime beer is best!'

or

'Alcohol is the pick you up that lets you down!'

A final note:- My remark about the anxiety of Plymouth mothers being alarmed that their daughters might take a sailor sweetheart might be misunderstood. In those days a sailor's pay was miserable and most served more than one term of two and a half years away on foreign stations. Nowadays deployments are usually three or six months and wives often fly out to join their husbands.

It was these factors that made marriage difficult. Furthermore, the poor pay was the cause of the Invergordon mutiny in 1931. Of course, Portsmouth and Chatham were in the same situation.

To old Navy men, the improved pay, women on ships and cooks wearing chefs' hats as at the Dorchester – all this seems to confirm the view that the modern Navy is really the grey funnel cruise line!

CHAPTER 43

The Royal Navy Today

The great ships and fleets we knew when I was young have sailed away into the mists of time. No more shall we see their splendid silhouettes, dark against the sunset. What a sense of security they gave us in those pre-war days!

The relinquishment of Empire and the huge technical advances in warship design and armament (missiles) mean that a modern frigate or destroyer can have greater firepower than all the sixteen-inch guns of the old Home Fleet. So, although numerically we are much weaker as a Naval power, the Royal Navy still packs a mighty nuclear punch, can still muster a surface force that is mobile in global terms, and, as the Falklands campaign showed, is still capable, with its indispensable Air Arm, of securing British interests. American benevolence and the presence of two carriers gave us victory, but it was a near thing. It could have ended in humiliation and disaster. The continuing reduction of our Naval Forces is a very grave mistake, for it renders triumph in a similar situation virtually impossible. In Naval terms we are at rock bottom. This is not, I suspect, merely a result of financial pressure by the Treasury in conflict with the Ministry of Defence.

I suspect that the real root of our decline as a Naval power is a loss of faith by our defence planners in the efficacy of large surface ships in this nuclear age. The Royal Navy, our traditional sure shield, has gone under the sea. Let us hope they are right!

Ah, but we, the ever shrinking survivors of the great old Royal Navy, can never forget those days when you could not turn a corner in our naval towns without a sight of Jack Tar and his twenty-six inch bell bottoms. Plymouth Hoe on a Sunday afternoon – sailors and girls everywhere!

And, how could we forget the mighty, so graceful, *Hood*, her sister battle cruisers, *Renown* and *Repulse* – such handsome, beautiful ships superior in their day to anything afloat! Then there were the old battle wagons of the Home and Mediterranean Fleets, *Barnham*, *Malaya*, *Resolution*, *Royal Sovereign*, *Warspite*, *Rodney*, *Nelson*, the tragic *Royal Oak* and the grand old *Revenge*. In my mind's eye I still see those smart County Class ten thousand-ton Cruisers, *Dorsetshire*, *Sussex*, *Shropshire*, *Cumberland* and *Cornwall* and others. Then there were 'The Boats', the old V & W Destroyers and the later post-World War I Destroyers, so sleek, the 'Maids of all work', busy little ships that could work in flotillas of eight or singly. Their work in two World Wars is well chronicled and earned them a unique reputation.

PART III

Record Promotion and the Music Business

CHAPTER 44

Record Promotion

At the end of the twenties and in the early thirties radio sets were coming into general use and the time soon came when almost every household possessed one.

This new medium, which took music into every home via the first London radio transmitter 2LO, caused great apprehension amongst the record companies, themselves just coming to terms with the successor to the primitive Hill and Dale cylinders. They feared that radio would kill their record sales. So they decided to huddle together for survival and formed *EMI, Electrical and Musical Industries*. The main labels were the famous *HMV, Columbia, Parlophone, Regal Zonophone* and some smaller firms.

Far from killing record sales, radio was to prove their salvation and usher in an era in which those sales rose to unbelievable heights. Nothing sells a record faster than a play over the airwaves, provided the sound appeals to the listener. This situation brought into being a band of men whose job it was to persuade disc jockeys and radio programme producers to include their latest new release in their broadcasts.

The sales of 78rpm records took a mighty leap forward as a consequence of the Rock & Roll revolution initiated by Elvis Presley, Buddy Holly, Eddie Cockrane, Bobby Vee and the all-conquering Beatles. These pioneers were swiftly followed by new talent, among whom the most prominent was the Rolling Stones. In their wake these guitar-led groups proliferated and some were very successful. Among other examples were 'The Who', 'Freddie and the Dreamers', 'Status Quo', 'The Electric Light Orchestra' and American groups of the quality of 'Canned Heat' and 'Credence Clearwater Revival'. There were many others, too numerous to mention.

Nor was this expansion of 78rpm discs confined to Rock. Solo artist singers sprang into the limelight of the calibre of Connie Francis, Eartha Kitt, Ella Fitzgerald, Rosemary Clooney, Marlene Dietrich, Alma Cogan, Barbara Streisand, Shirley Bassey, Petula Clark, Dusty Springfield and others, and the Americans, Doris Day, Cher, Debbie Reynolds and Julie London. This is to mention but a few.

Male singers too achieved enormous sales. Frank Sinatra, Bing Crosby,

Action Man! The author at the Promo Desk, UA Records.

Andy Williams, Nat King Cole, Johnny Mathis, to name but the most eminent. Country singers too shared in the single sales bonanza: Hank Williams, Jim Reeves, Slim Whitman.

Volume sales came also from the big bands, Glen Miller, Duke Ellington, Benny Goodman, Ray Conniff, the German band of James Last, Andre Kostelarnetz, Russ Morgan. We must include the British bands of earlier times, purveyors of sweet dance music, Ray Noble, Geraldo, Roy Fox, Ambrose, Henry Hall, Jay Wilbur, Joe Loss and the hugely popular Mantovani.

These artists created a turnover beyond the wildest dreams of the earlier record companies, and all these single records had to fight to gain the airtime needed to launch them on their sales success.

The amount of airtime allowed to the BBC is controlled by an agreement with the powerful Musicians Union, designed to protect the jobs of live musicians. In any one day, only a limited number of records can be broadcast, so here the record promotions man finds his challenge. The firm that employs him expects to see their catalogue well represented on station play lists. Competition is intense. All major firms have record promotions

Record promotion man! The author outside the BBC, Langham Place.

men, and the company's latest singles by important artists are expected to gain a place on the main record shows.

The promotions man survives by the quality of his relationships with the big disc jockeys and radio producers. Over time he must gain their respect and confidence, so that when he tells them a new release is on the move in the shops, they believe him.

It is all far more than just dropping a new record on a DJ's or radio producer's desk. The promotions man must be fully familiar with the record he is pushing. He must not try to inflict a record on a DJ which is out of character with the show's format. He must be able to give detailed information about the music, the lyrics and the artist, for this helps the programme builder to write his script.

It is not only the main national programmes of the BBC that the promotions man is responsible for; he has to deal also with the important regional stations, Glasgow, Cardiff, Belfast and Dublin, as well as the private commercial stations, the chief of these in former times being Radio Luxembourg – alas no more.

Times have changed and some of the most valuable programmes, such as 'Housewives Choice', and the wonderful 'Sunday Family Favourites' broadcast from London by the inimitable Ms. Jean Metcalf, and Bill Crozier in Cologne, are no more; they are victims of a much changed Britain.

Some fifteen million listeners used to join in what was a very happy record party each Sunday at midday. It was a request show for service men and families in Germany and their relatives home in Britain, a prime target for the promotions men. A play on Two-Way Family Favourites would, if the record was right, ensure a big sales movement early the following week.

Sometimes referred to by the ill-informed as 'pluggers' or 'exploitation men', these record men were the weekly mendicants seeking support from David Jacobs, Peter Murray, Tony Blackburn, Jimmy Young, Brian Mathews, Ed Stewart, Jimmy Savile and others.

Each week around 50 to 70 new single records issued by the various companies all struggled for a place on the play lists. Most were doomed to perish, for only a small number could find a place in the record programmes. It can easily be seen what a high degree of tact was needed in making weekly approaches to these DJ's and producers, submerged as they were in a pile of new issues. Careful timing and restraint were needed; otherwise you irritated these men by calling or ringing at the wrong time. I once rang a well-known DJ when he was at dinner. He froze me out for about three months. I met him in a corridor of the BBC and said, 'Mea culpa'. He smiled, said nothing, but put my Connie Francis's 'Who's sorry

Miss Connie Francis of 'Who's Sorry Now?' fame.

now' in three times in the following couple of weeks. I learned my lesson!

There were just a handful of top promotions men. I knew them well and name them here with pleasure: Johnny Wise – Pye Records, Tony Hall – Decca, Paddy Fleming – Philips Records, Don Agness – Leeds Music, John Phillips and Harry Waters – EMI – and I could not forget that irrepressible Irishman, Tommy Loftus of RCA Records.

We travelled and socialised a lot and made fortunes for artists and record companies.

A 'hit' we used to say, 'has many fathers'. A miss was always the fault of the promotions man, who had failed to secure sufficient exposure! No one, especially the golden boys of the record industry, the A and R men who actually made the records in the studio, would ever admit that such a 'miss' was a bad record! An A and R man could remove a promotions man.

It was interesting to note how a couple of plays on the air could send a new disc roaring up the Top Twenty charts. In other cases, however, a big 'hit' sometimes took weeks or even months to break through. Such a one was Don McLean's huge seller, 'American Pie'. A hit in the States, we were expected to make it a top ten record in the UK market. It would not budge and most DJ's avoided it like the plague. The lyric was, to UK ears, odd, and I sought clarification from our American associates and circulated their explanation to all DJ's and producers. Still weeks passed and it did not move. That Prince of DJ's, Alan Freeman, and his producer, Denys Jones, shared my belief that it was a 'hit' record. Alan's show was *Pick of the Pops*, a major spot in the week's programmes.

Week after week I told Alan and Denys, 'No, it's not moving, but please, Gentlemen, stay with it'. After 11 weeks Denys told me it would have to be removed from the play list if it did not show immediate signs of life. It did! I rang the wholesalers who said, 'It's away!' ... And, it was a MONSTER.

Don McLean followed this success with that lovely song, 'Vincent', inspired by the painter, Vincent van Gogh. Don is a modern natural troubadour, who once played and sang to passengers on the Mississippi river boats. He has many fine songs to his credit.

It is just over seven decades ago that, as boys, my brother Billy and I watched our father fiddle with a small piece of wire, attaching it to a crystal, and – hey presto – through the earphones he placed upon our infant heads we heard music! We used to go to bed with those earphones on our heads and go to sleep to the music of Ambrose or Jack Hylton, or some other of the several fine dance bands of that era. Our aerial hung from an inverted broom!

What, I wonder, would our great grandfather, a shepherd in the Cambridgeshire village of Tydd St Giles, have thought about that primitive radio receiver? Or what would his reaction have been to the miracle of the now almost obsolete CD, where, by disc, you are holding a great orchestral performance of a complete Beethoven symphony?

I suspect Grandfather would have hurried back to the silent and beautiful solitude of his sheep!

Incidentally, reverting for a moment to the Don McLean 'Vincent' record, Vincent van Gogh lodged in a house exactly opposite the entrance to the playground of my school in Brixton, South West London. A plaque sits over the front door where this great artist lived.

I never noticed, for in those days I was addicted to catapults and conkers rather than the resident of an undistinguished little terraced house.

CHAPTER 45

The Meeting

It was a momentous day, a day that would change Western society for ever, a day that would stand Britain on its head.

The occasion was a routine 798 rpm.Repertoire Planning Meeting, in the course of which each of the A&R Men would be presenting the proposed new releases to the Repertoire Meeting for audition and approval. New single 78 rpm records were released weekly.

For those unfamiliar with the recording industry, I should explain that 'A&R' stands for 'Artistes and Repertoire'. The A&R men, therefore, were those golden ones who put together artist and song or other performance and who carried responsibility for the final sound created in the recording studio. These important fellows were highly skilled in their choices of artistes and in what went into the grooves of the plastic disc.

The A&R men usually controlled substantial budgets, from which they had to meet recording costs in the studio. In their search for talent and material, they were required to socialize and cultivate artistes and their agents.

I never met an A&R man who would admit that he had made a bad record! To them, their latest recording was the ultimate musical achievement, a certainty for the Top Twenty in the charts of the musical papers. No – if their record flopped (they often did!) it was because the Promotion Man had failed to gain sufficient exposure. The Promo Men were, and doubtless still are, the whipping boys of the record business. I know!

My job was easier that that of the other A&R men, for I was not competent to work with recording engineers. My function was to audition and select single and long-playing records from the important MGM catalogue. Miss Connie Francis gained a huge success with 'Who's Sorry Now', still a frequent item on radio. My good luck it was to have many of the great musicals in my sphere of activity. MGM had several significant chart successes in my time.

Let me revert to that Repertoire Meeting held in the early 50's in the EMI Offices at Great Castle Street, London W1. On this historic day (though we knew not its significance at the time), the following were present: The Chief Executive of EMI Records, Sir Joseph Lockwood, Walter

Connie Francis with the author.

Ridley of HMV, Norman Newall (also a talented lyricist) representing Columbia Records, George Martin, Parlophone, of Beatles fame, that fine orchestra leader and delightful personality, Norrie Paramour, and myself carrying the flag of America's celebrated MGM Record Division.

A record from our American licensor, RCA Records, lay on the table and was duly presented by Walter Ridley, for HMV were the RCA outlet in the UK. The reaction was unusual. Everyone was puzzled, bewildered and quite unable to comprehend the exciting but – to our ears – utterly strange sounds that we were hearing. This, it must be remembered, was the era of sweet dance music, straight vocalists like Ruby Murray and singers of the calibre of Doris Day, Shirley Bassey, Petula Clark and 'Dusty' Springfield. It was the era of Frank Sinatra, Paul Anka and Bing Crosby. They were the messengers of sweet romance, quite unlike the vibrant, intense, rhythmic frenzy of the new Rock sound, which, inside a decade, brought with it degradation and the drug culture which ravages our young people today.

The meeting was inclined to reject that record. It was, however, causing enormous interest in America and so, in deference to our American associates, release was approved – reluctantly!

And what was the title and who was the artist that had so baffled the EMI Committee?

It was 'Heartbreak Hotel' *by that musical revolutionary, Elvis Presley*!

The EMI wise men at that meeting should not be too harshly judged. Our ears were attuned to a totally different sound world. We were living with Ambrose, Jack Hylton, Geraldo, Henry Hall, Roy Fox, Debroy Somers. Pre-Presley, our own indigenous popular vocalists were Gracie Fields, George Formby, Sir Harry Lauder and Will Fyfe. These artistes, together with the great American icons mentioned above, conditioned us to a less frenetic and more civilized musical culture. Alas! It was too boring for our '60's young people.

A short postscript may be added to this story. American friends told me that 'Heartbreak Hotel' nearly went to a fine American artist named Carl Perkins, but that at the time he was unable to visit the recording studio because of an indisposition. If Carl had recorded that song, the history of Western society might well have turned out differently. However, I cannot vouch for the accuracy of the story.

Yet though Elvis Presley was the catalyst of a social and musical revolution, it would be unjust to attribute to him the responsibility for the era of decadence which followed. Elvis set the ball rolling, a ball kicked merrily along by those other pioneers of the Rock movement, Eddie Cochran, Buddy Holly and Bobby Vee. Together with Elvis, and soon to be joined by the mighty Beatles and the Rolling Stones, they gave the young fine melodies married to romantic lyrics. All this was carried along by the 'beat' which, in the young, created an urge to dance themselves into a frenzy.

It was this frenzy called Rock and Roll which later spawned monster groups (encouraged throughout by a heedless media), whose ugly noises and innuendo-laden lyrics (often shockingly ungrammatical) filled the minds of highly vulnerable young people with a false and distorted set of values. Rampant hedonism replaced conventional morality. As a result, instead of young girls learning how to value themselves, promiscuity is nowadays represented as the norm.

Those big bad groups were, as they still are today, the troubadours of 'Political Correctness'. Their venues are the squalid discos and clubs in which many a young life has been soiled, or even worse, destroyed. The outcome has been a million children without fathers, a high incidence of sexually contracted diseases and a host of young victims of a PC (politically correct) educational establishment. Hence those involved have been deprived of the wonder and beauty of the world they live in. This is the legacy of the diabolical union which has been forged between the PC virus and the dregs of the Rock revolution.

May the Lord have pity on us all!

CHAPTER 46

Happy Birthdays

The Ike and Tina Turner Revue sprang into international fame after they accompanied the Rolling Stones on a major European tour in the early '70's.

A part of this acclaimed act were three beautiful Afro-American girls called the Ikettes. Chosen for their beauty and talent as dancers, they were delightful young ladies with a mischievous sense of humour; they loved a joke.

A couple of days before we were due in Munich, the girls said to me: 'It's Ike's birthday in Munich and you know we are going to have a big party. You, Ronnie, have got to help us give Ike a *surprise!* You are going to be an "Ikette".' 'How can I do that?' I replied. 'I'm ugly, can't dance, and besides I'm the wrong sex.' 'Never mind all that', they said, 'We've got a dress for you and a nice wig and we'll teach you to dance.'

I rehearsed with them a simple dance routine, three to the right, three to the left and then a 180 degree turn and da capo, same again.

In Munich, in the very pleasant Hilton Hotel, arrangements were in hand to give Ike a big celebration. Gerhardt from our German office was Master of Ceremonies and at the right moment announced a special performance by *The Ikettes!* The music played and in we Ikettes danced. I felt a bit like Margot Fonteyn just before solos – very wound up. To much laughter, we did our dance and I tossed a piece of paper into Ike's lap with room number 247 on it.

After the party Ike said to me, 'Ronnie, you are the ugliest Ikette I have ever seen!' I could not argue with that.

Next year it was Miss Turner's birthday in the same city and in the same hotel. Before Munich we were in Vienna for a concert.

In the afternoon there was a conference for the Austrian press and this was arranged to take place at a studio close to our hotel. So, as it was but a few minutes walk, Ike, Tina and their personal assistant Rhonda Graam set off and soon we found ourselves in the famous Kärtner Strasse, Vienna's Bond Street, a woman's paradise of splendid shops selling expensive jewellery and the very latest ladies' fashions.

As we passed one of these shops, the sort of place swiftly to empty a

94

Tina Turner and the Ikettes.

husband's wallet, Miss Turner stopped in her tracks, bewitched by a lovely three-piece lavender-coloured ensemble (I hope that is the right term!). She moved to enter and buy it but Ike called, 'Come on, we are late, come back later,' so Tina moved reluctantly on.

I knew the Company United Artists Records would approve my giving Miss Turner a birthday present, so when the party moved on, I darted back and bought the object of Tina's desire. Just as I was about to leave, I caught a glimpse of Tina heading back at high speed to the shop. Just in time, I persuaded the lady in the shop to hide me in a back room, as it was imperative that I should not be seen. Otherwise the surprise planned for Munich would have failed.

Miss Turner asked for her heart's desire and was abashed when the lady explained, 'Oh Madam, I'm so sorry, but that suit is *sold!*'

In Munich, when the party was in full swing, I stole up to where Tina was sitting and said, 'Miss Turner, please accept this small gift from all at United Artists London and Los Angeles'. She opened it and an expression of pure delight appeared on her face. I never saw a happier lady.

'Ronnie,' Miss Turner said, 'you've socked it to me!' It was one of my memorable moments!

'Flower Power'. Ron Bell as promotions man, UA Records visits Johnny Beerling, then head of BBC Radio 1.

CHAPTER 47

Ike and Tina in Berlin

Ike and Tina Turner again. On leaving the aircraft, we always tried to ensure that nothing was left in the 'plane. On this occasion, driving in the limousine to the hotel, Ike suddenly grabbed my arm. 'My bag!' he exclaimed, I must have left it in the aircraft.' Mr Turner always carried his own hand luggage in a special bag, which never left his person. It contained vital travel documents and cash. The car stopped and I caught a taxi to hasten back to the airport, at once making my way to the British Airways desk.

Mr Turner's bag contained the takings of several recent concerts within its leather sides. Many thousands of US dollars were involved. I asked the girl at the desk if anything had been handed in and my heart went cold when she said, 'No, nothing has been handed in'. I gulped and requested her to check back to the aircraft. 'Please check again, Miss, it is very important.' She picked up a 'phone and I looked despondently around the circular-shaped BA desk. I noticed a strap hanging down from a rack under the counter. 'May I see that please, Miss?'; I pointed to the strap. It was Ike's bag! After satisfying her that it was in order for me to collect the bag, I checked the contents, got into a taxi and sped to the hall, where Ike was doing a sound check. He was on stage and I held the bag aloft . . . He saw it and did a victory roll in the middle of a guitar solo.

CHAPTER 48

Ike Turner

A word in Ike Turner's favour is long overdue. He wasn't the 'cruel and manipulative' person that he has been described as. I worked closely with Mr and Mrs Turner for four years, travelling everywhere with them in the same car on their long and exhausting European tours in the 'seventies.

Like most of us, Ike is no angel. But he wasn't cruel and was no more manipulative than anyone else with artistic and professional responsibilities.

On a long and tiring journey en route from Munich to Salzburg, our driver was asked to turn off the road so that we could get some rest and refreshment. In a typical Austrian inn in a remote village we encountered a mentally disabled young man crouched in a corner seat, gazing at us with wild eyes.

He was terribly retarded and the innkeeper told us how his mother, who had cared for him, had recently died. Ike Turner was visibly moved and left a considerable sum of money with the innkeeper to buy clothes and necessities for him.

Then in the Kärtnerstrasse in Vienna, where Ike and Tina were admiring the precious objects on display in a jewellers, he spontaneously bought her an expensive piece of jewellery. He could be a martinet to the band and crew on tour, but he often displayed great generosity.

He was very kind to me and always gave me, and others in the crew, a parting gift. Miss Turner I remember as a warm, kind and superbly professional lady. On stage she sizzled, but I always felt she longed for the fierce demands of her tours to end so that she could be a devoted mother and housewife – not a bit like the fiery megastar she is today. In the course of my duties, sometimes waiting with a dressing-gown to usher her off stage and into her dressing room, I never saw a mark or bruise on her magnificent torso.

Ike with Tina celebrating the award of a silver disc for Nutbush City Limits. *Ron Bell made the presentation.*

CHAPTER 49

Ike and Tina in Rome

Ike and Tina Turner's musicians were checking in at the elegant Hilton Hotel, which stands, or rather perches, on a hill. Among them were two very black young players from Los Angeles. The Head of Reception looked at them and signalled that he wanted to speak. I sensed a problem and so it turned out to be — a very serious one. 'We are overbooked,' said this suave and polished character. 'How can that possibly be?' I rejoined. 'I have your confirmation for the Ike and Tina party here in my bag.'

It was to no avail. 'I am sorry,' said the Head of Reception, 'I cannot take them.' Mr Turner was rightly very angry. 'Either these musicians stay with us,' he said, 'or the Rome concert will be cancelled'. Now, I wondered, what is to be done to avoid a grave financial loss and disappointment to several hundred fans? I took a seat in the lounge and bought a beer, trying to think of a solution. Two young American businessmen sat at the next table and one said pleasantly, 'You look worried'. I gave him the facts and, after a few words with his friend, he said: 'Look, if you can find us two comparable rooms in another hotel, we will move out and then you have our two rooms for your guys.' I was touched by their kindness and desire to help (I suspect they wanted to strike a blow against racism!) and shot off fast to a 'phone. I soon found two singles in the prestigious Excelsior.

Now to the dénouement. I informed the Hilton man that there were now two rooms available and that I expected that the problem was now resolved. A darkness came over his Latin face and for a moment I thought he was still going to reject our musicians, both now weary and disconsolate and very black. I had one of those sudden flashes of inspiration which lucky fellows like me sometimes experience and this, I believe, swung the affair to a happy conclusion. I told him journalists from major American papers were attending the concert and would it not reflect very badly on the Hilton if the concert were to be cancelled by the hotel? 'Let them sign the register,' he said.

I was able to phone Mr Turner and tell him his men were safely in their rooms. 'How did you do it?' he asked. 'It was my Guardian Angel,' I replied. Then I told him about his two young compatriots. Delightful chaps those young Americans. I hope today they are heads of vast corporations. Obviously my Guardian Angel is an Ike and Tina fan.

Miss Tina Turner and Ike on stage.

CHAPTER 50

Scalped!

The concert promoter gave a party for the Ike and Tina Revue and for the local media, TV, Radio and Press.

We were in a large room on the top floor of an hotel in the Kürfürstendam, Berlin, and it appeared to me that this was going to be an all-male affair.

Whilst we were sipping our drinks and chatting in a mixture of English and German, a large door opened and a flurry of scantily dressed young ladies descended upon us and distributed themselves among the surprised guests.

A natural puritan, I was at first prepared to be indignant at this intrusion, but I confess I found the experience very delightful and I struggled hard against a feeling of guilt. In my mind's eye I saw my sweet wife, and that was the cause of some discomfiture!

Soon I found myself gazing into a pair of very blue eyes. She was a real Teuton beauty, the sort that would have sent composer Richard Wagner into an emotional freefall. Without any warning, this shameless but heavenly creature leaned forward and in one swift movement she swept off my 'topper' (hairpiece) exposing my billiard-ball cranium to all present. A horrific moment of humiliation! 'Da bist Du, Opah!' she said (There you are, Grandpa) as I hoped the earth would swallow me up. She must have known I was just eligible to enter the SAGA fold!

One man however was outraged. Mr Ike Turner demanded the immediate removal of the girl concerned. Mrs Turner was not present.

After all this uproar, a mixture of hilarity and anger on the part of my party companions, I saw in a kind of vision my wife Peggy saying to me: 'Serves you right, you silly old fool.'

Ah! But those eyes were so very, very blue!

For a moment, looking into them had put me in the presence of Valhalla and the Gods!

Ike and Tina in Rome.

CHAPTER 51

Paul Anka

Paul Anka is a legend of our time. He ranks with the highest achievers in the popular music of our era. As a vocalist, he stands among the greats and can be mentioned in the same context as Bing Crosby and Frank Sinatra. As a composer and lyricist, his songs have gone round the world. His contributions to the entertainment industry have earned him innumerable awards and a recognition that is all but unique. For example, the French Government awarded him the title, 'Chevalier in the Order of Arts and Letters', and he is among only a handful of Americans to have received this prestigious award. Recently the National Academy of Popular Music elected him into The Songwriter's Hall of Fame.

He has several million best-sellers to his credit. 'Diana' was said to have been inspired when an au pair girl of that name, employed in the Anka household, captivated a very young Paul. This wonderful song, with its romantic plea, 'Stay with me, Diana', conquered the world.

An equally significant success, which became a world 'hit' and will endure as a part of peoples' lives, is 'I Did It My Way'. The lyric is magnificent and builds steadily to reach a dramatic emotional climax. Both Frank Sinatra and Paul Anka gave unforgettable performances and achieved hit records for posterity. The melody of this song inspired Mr Anka's wonderful lyric. It was by the French singer and composer, Claude Francois, who died in a tragic accident in which he was electrocuted in his bath.

As a performer, Paul Anka is a perfectionist. He once told me, 'When people buy a ticket to one of my shows, I am absolutely committed to giving them my very best effort. I must give them my "all"'. I never met an artist with so strong a sense of obligation towards his audience. And hereby hangs a tale.

In Hamburg, Mr Anka was scheduled for an important television special in the famous Congress Hall. We did not realise it at the time, but it was part of normal procedure in this part of Germany to admit ticket-buying members of the public to rehearsals. My company ought to have been aware of this unusual, but perfectly proper, method of subsidising production costs. However, in the USA and Britain such a practice is unknown.

Paul Anka.

When Mr Anka became aware that the public would be admitted to his rehearsal, he was appalled. 'When I rehearse,' he told me, 'I may want to dress informally, take a break, repeat a part of my act or stop for refreshment. At rehearsal I cannot give my best, and those who bought tickets must have their money refunded. My rehearsal must be private, without the public.' It was an ultimatum. For some time it seemed he might withdraw, with the result that a substantial financial loss would fall upon the promoters, among whom was my own Record Company. Crisis!

Our salvation came via the good offices of NDR (North German Radio), who kindly broadcast throughout the day before the TV concert, and a steady stream of people attended to return tickets and collect reimbursements from long trestle tables that were provided.

As for the performance itself, Paul Anka was superb and the Germans gave him an ovation.

If you work with Paul Anka, you must be as he is, 100% professional. A few days later I myself made a serious *faux pas*. It was at Heathrow Airport.

To my horror, I saw Mr Anka wheeling a trolley piled high with his own and Mrs Anka's personal luggage and heading for the Concorde departure lounge. I was too late to help them.

I fully and painfully realised that, courteous and considerate man as he was, I had failed him as a professional. At the time my letter of apology and explanation was returned. He had dropped me like a hot potato! Happily all that is past history, and with characteristic generosity, he has now fully forgiven me.

CHAPTER 52

Cannes and Nice

Cannes might reasonably be described as Europe's Las Vegas. The casinos are a mecca for the gambling set from all over the world and Cannes is also host to two important annual festivals.

The first of these is the International Record and Music Publishing Market Festival, Midem, which facilitates contacts between companies from all over the world, as a consequence of which there have been countless fruitful exchanges of talent and repertoire, and a cross-fertilization of ideas and songs which would otherwise never have been achieved.

The second big Festival is, of course, the International Film Festival, which performs an identical service for the Film Industry.

These festivals enrich these two towns on the Riviera, and hotels such as the Majestic and the Carlton now give hospitality to VIPs from the music and film industries. These hotels were one of the favourite haunts of rich Victorians, after whom the Promenade des Anglais takes its name. Lined with palm trees, this famous road skirts wonderful beaches, where in good weather the beautiful young people surrender their torsos to the sun god. A place for hedonists, Cannes' temptations are many and there is also a mafia! I met two of the gentlemen belonging to it.

There was an Ike and Tina concert about half an hour's drive from Cannes. It was a sell-out, which was fortunate for our company, who were co-sponsors responsible for half the promotional and tour expenses.

The worst part of any tour manager's job, I believe, is to collect the money from ticket sales. In cases where the relationship between promoter and record company is well established, there are usually no problems, but where the local promoter is new and unknown to record company and artists' management, there is some risk. And, so it was on this occasion. The contract stipulated that receipts should be handed over before commencement of the second part of the concert. I duly presented myself, but was fobbed off with smiles and cups of tea. They said, 'We're busy just now, but don't worry, we'll settle soon.'

I could have kept our artists off stage, but I felt that was not a good solution for there would have been uproar in the hall. 'When', I enquired, 'do you intend paying according to contract?' More prevarication: 'Come to the office after the show', they said, 'and we'll settle'.

I presented myself, but still received no money.

I saw the two men concerned, one a Korean, getting into a car and realised they were off with the takings! I followed in our company car, and, after some ten minutes they stopped and entered a restaurant, where they sat down at a table for dinner. I decided to wait until they had eaten and then to approach them. I had no chance to do that for one of them, a large, but seemingly affable man, came to where I sat and said, 'Come and join us for a drink'. I thought 'At last, they are going to hand over the money!'

Oh no! The big fellow, leaning across the table, said, 'Go back to your hotel. There is no money, there will be no money.' I got the message, drank the brandy they bought me and returned to the hotel.

I called my Managing Director at about 2.00am UK time and gave him the news . . . a considerable loss for our company. 'Get some sleep, Ron', he said. 'There is nothing we can do'.

A nice way to spend an evening!

CHAPTER 53

Amsterdam in the Mid-Seventies

Canned Heat, based in Los Angeles, California, was one of the top bands around throughout the '70's and their blues-based sound won them many fans in many countries.

Each one a fine musician, they loved what they did and big Bob Hite was said to have the finest collection of blues records outside the Library of Congress.

'On the Road Again' and 'Going up the Country' were big single records that made the charts in Britain and America.

They called me their 'British Freak', which I took as a compliment. Agreeable fellows they were, who liked to enjoy themselves after concerts, and nothing gave them greater pleasure than to stroll around some new city and enjoy its sights and hospitality.

They had strong Californian accents and were amused by my English manners and accent. They used to call me 'old chap', whilst I revenged myself by saying 'man' as often as opportunity arose.

One afternoon around 5 pm we piled into a van and found ourselves on a trip to a place about half an hour from Amsterdam. Here an open-air concert was to be held and the venue was on an improvised stage set in a kind of grotto surrounded by trees. Inside the grotto was a mini-Roman Coliseum seating three or four hundred. The advancing night was countered by brilliant white lights suspended along the trees, and the band played before a full house of young Dutch people, who, I suspect, were already aware of what the evening was to hold for them.

It was a splendid nocturnal occasion. The scene was so brilliantly lit up, it was brighter than natural daylight. The youngsters enjoyed themselves and they looked happy in shirts and tops in all the colours of the rainbow. They cheered and stamped their feet as Canned Heat roared through 'On the Road Again', 'Bullfrog Blues', 'Rollin and Tumblin', 'Time Was', 'Boogie Music' and other numbers.

We were in a kind of Dutch fairyland. That highly disciplined, exciting instrumental group filled the night air with rich tones and driving rhythmic accompaniments that had the young audience swaying in their seats, clapping hands and cheering wildly.

Canned Heat.

I wonder what the old Dutch sea dogs and great artists of long ago would have made of it all.

In Amsterdam the next day I was taken to a deconsecrated church, then a venue for rock concerts. I walked through this once holy place and saw groups of young people under the influence of cannabis, comatose and sprawled, some twenty or so, all across the floor. It reeked!

In Amsterdam, with its canals and barges, abundant pubs and cafés, I suspected the Dutch thoroughly enjoyed their decadence. They all seemed very happy!

I met 'Canned Heat' at the airport and greeted them with the following diatribe:-

'It is my pleasure, privilege and duty to welcome you on behalf of United Artists Records and to convey you to your hotel. If I had my way, however, I would convey you rebellious colonials to the dungeons of the Tower of London!'

Loud laughter and instant rapport!

CHAPTER 54

Fonograf. A World-Class Group from Hungary

Line-up:-

Levente Szörényi	Lead vocal, guitar
János Bródy	Steel guitar
Lászó Tolcsvoy	Banjo, Harmonica, Keyboards
Mihály Móricz	Guitar
Szaóbolcs Szörényi	Bass
Oszkór Német	Drums, Percussion

Fonograf is basically a vocal formation with a special style which can be called Country and Eastern Rock.

To say that Fonograf is popular in the Eastern bloc would be an understatement. The songs composed by the members of the group make up about 25% of record sales in Hungary and they have also composed film music with great success. Their overall record sales of songs penned by the song-writing team of Brody/Szörényi have reached more than two million in Hungary alone, and these two names are responsible for more than two hundred successful melodies, 21 LP's for the Group, and also 'Hit' numbers for the very successful Hungarian singer, Miss Zsuzso Koncz.

Fonograf strives to create a new pattern of popular music: Country and Eastern Rock. They have not had the success in the West that their immense talent deserves. This, despite sustained promotional efforts by United Artists Records, England. The explanation for this relative failure is the enormous pressure on air time imposed by the huge number of top-flight Western artists, whose collective output of weekly new single records serves virtually to exclude newcomers to the British market, and this problem imposes similar difficulties on new indigenous talent too. To break through this fiercely competitive market requires not just efficient promotion, which Fonograf would concede they have received, but a huge slice of that rare commodity, *luck*!

If Fonograf had originated in the West, their talent as composers and brilliant musicians would have carried them to the summit of success in popular music.

111

Fonograf, the Ace Hungarian Group, Budapest Studio, 1978.

'Greyhound' and 'Lonesome Once Again', with lyrics by talented Yorkshire lady Stacey Wilde were, and remain, top-ten songs.

CHAPTER 55

The Bonzo Dog Band

In the decade of the 'sixties we became aware, as never before, of the mysteries of outer space. This was the consequence of NASA's exploits and the media coverage that followed. The fact that a man had actually been on the moon seized the imagination of almost everyone on our earth and the speculation about other civilisations 'out there' continues to this day.

It was perhaps inevitable that the phenomenon of Space should engage the attention of, and inspire, a group of talented young men in Britain, who burst upon the music scene bearing the title, 'The Bonzo Dog Band'.

It was both the good fortune and the privilege of Liberty-United Artists Records to sign and promote these gifted entertainers, all with academic backgrounds. They were a delight to work with and highly amusing.

Eccentric and, as I used to think, slightly insane, though in the nicest possible way, they ushered in a new sound and an act which was both aurally and visually compelling.

The main driving force in a band utterly different from any of its contemporaries consisted of three highly talented individuals, Messrs Stanshall, Spear and Innes. The Bonzos were originals, bizarre in dress and sound alike. After a slow start, their 'Urban Spaceman' shot up the charts like a NASA rocket. In that single compelling single, with its irresistible beat, there was something of outer space itself. It drove the record along at an exciting pace, a little like a ride on a missile – and enormous fun! Today the record is still as valid as it was all those years ago. That group made, I believe, two LP's. In the music of the Bonzos the spirit of the 'sixties is enshrined. Each member was a strong individualist in his own right and hence it was, perhaps, inevitable that before long they would disband and each depart to make an impact in television and the theatre.

Although quite different musically, the Bonzos made me recall a clever Swedish band of long ago called 'The Sputniks'. They were inspired by the Russian astronauts.

I wonder whether, in their leisure time in space, the crews of Star War ships listen to the 'Bonzo Dog Band'.

I would not be surprised.

CHAPTER 56

The Seekers

One day in the early sixties there came through the doors of Oriole Records in New Bond Street, London, three stalwart young men and a pretty girl. They were The Seekers! At that time unknown in Britain, they were keen to enter the British market and were sent to us by their Australian record company, Festival, with whom Oriole had a contractual relationship.

To promote a new and unknown act requires a considerable investment. Advertising, studio costs, entertaining and transport all involve expenditure and outlay which, if the new act fails, would incur, for a small company, an unacceptable financial loss. So this wonderful vocal quartet slipped through our hands and was signed by EMI. The rest is history. 'The Seekers' achieved huge sales with unforgettable performances of wonderful songs, some of which I give below.

'I'll Never Find Another You'
'A World of our Own'
'The Carnival is Over'
'Blowin' in the Wind'
'Lemon Tree'

There were, of course, many others, including 'Waltzing Matilda'. Today they survive strongly in an age of frenetic popular music. For those who seek vocal excellence, if they are not in your collection, track them down in your local record shop.

Miss Judy Durham's voice is of stunning beauty. She ranks at the very top of female singers. It is a fact that The Seekers is the best vocal quartet in the world of popular music.

Some readers may recognise the famous Russian traditional song, 'Stenka Razin' in its western dress as 'The Carnival is Over'. Stenka Razin was a 17th century Cossack bandit who was foolish enough to lead a revolt against the Czar. He was executed in 1692 but we should all be grateful to him for inspiring this lovely, haunting melody. Today he is still a hero present in many Russian ballads.

You can hear Stenka Razin sung by the Red Army Choir on HMV 12" LP Number ASD.3200.

CHAPTER 57

Bobby Vee

When the final history of the Rock and Roll revolution is told, Robert Velline, internationally known as Bobby Vee, will stand side by side with the illustrious founder fathers of a music that was to sweep the young off their feet and change Western society forever.

Bobby Vee's success came fast and early. He was but a sixteen year-old schoolboy from Fargo, North Dakota, with his own band, when he stepped in at short notice to fill the gap left by that tragic air crash which robbed the musical world of the talents of Buddy Holly and Ritchie Valens. That tragedy in Iowa brought young Bobby before the audience at Moorhead and this concert proved to be the catalyst for his meteoric rise to international fame.

Bobby Vee songs are unique. Examine closely the lyrics and you will find that they marry genuine romantic sentiment, based on true romance, with fine melodies, the vehicles of the new Rock and Roll style; of course, all this with that irresistible rhythmic fascination.

The titles convey the essence of the songs: 'Take good care of my baby' reveals concern by a young man for his girl, 'Rubber Ball' undiluted youthful exuberance and fun, 'The night has a thousand eyes' is a Rock and Roll masterpiece, 'Run to him' and 'Come back when you grow up' are wise words to an over-eager, but too young, lady. These are wonderful Rock and Roll classics, which will be heard as long as there is popular music in the Rock and Roll style.

Rock stars live fast and furious lives and many fall by the wayside. Bobby Vee still has his schooldays sweetheart, who has been his wife for more than thirty-five years, and he has three fine sons, Jeff, Tom and Robb, and a daughter Jennifer. Bobby has kept on an even keel in the very stormy waters of the popular music scene. He is a role model for all young music fans, whom he still delights at some 100 concerts a year with his sons, *The Vee Band*.

There is something important to tell non-Americans about Bobby Vee. The state of North Dakota has a very special award, given only to citizens whose achievements attain worldwide recognition.

Recently, June 1999, Governor Ed Shafer presented to Bobby this hugely

Bobby Vee (second from right), Mrs Vee and family.

Bobby Vee, the pioneer Rock star, visits United Artists Records Office in London.

prestigious award known as 'The Theodore Roosevelt Rough Rider Award', the highest honour within the State Governor's gift. A legend of our time and a true American gentleman is Bobby Vee.

PART IV

Great Music

CHAPTER 58

The Deity and Beethoven

It is ten pm on a Saturday. One senses that weariness that sometimes makes itself felt at the end of a long week. It is over! Clasping my glass, I sink into a mood of philosophical reflection. In the papers one reads such terrible tales of human cruelty and folly. How cruel and pointless it seems! How hard it is to believe in a merciful God who allows such deeds of wickedness! Yet, as I grow ever nearer to that great harbour in the sky, I am convinced there *is* a God. I accept the theory put forward by the Jesuits, namely that the fact that we are capable of the concept of a Deity, all-powerful and eternal, must mean there is one. If it were a false concept, that would mean that we mortals created Him and that is a nonsense. This little item of theology might not be enough for most people, but there are many, many more obvious proofs of His existence.

The ebb and flow of tides, the glorious galaxies that live and die in myriads, existing for aeons, then fading away like phantom adumbrations of the divine scheme; how wondrous the concepts of infinity of time and space!

How varied and beautiful are the fauna and vegetation of our planet! Perceive the structure of a rose or the colours of a butterfly and ask yourself: 'Could all this be an accident? An effect without a cause?' All these mind-boggling phenomena are expressed in great art and in music, especially that of the Titan, L. von Beethoven.

It was my father who brought me to the music of Beethoven. Around the age of sixteen, I was moved to near-ecstasy by a joyous performance of the Ninth Symphony, especially Schiller's 'Ode to Joy' in the finale. I stumbled out of the concert hall bemused and exalted. Sometimes I feel that the whole of the human ordeal is embraced in the main subject of the adagio. This theme, so pregnant with noble humanity and hope, comes like a stab of dazzling white light to illuminate a world often dark and desolate. 'Alle Männer werden Brüder,' proclaims this music. All men shall be brothers! When, oh when? The barbarities of Serbs, Israelis, Croats and the IRA, among others, mock the Schiller and Beethoven dream. Of course, not all can find the certainty of God through Beethoven; each must seek his own path through his own experience of art and love – in short, through his own eyes, ears and emotions. Some, I suppose, will arrive at the truth via Michael Jackson or Tina Turner.

Beethoven's nine symphonies contain the ultimate in inspiration. Through the years I have learned these symphonies and know almost every bar. Wherever I am, and at any time, I can enjoy my own concert.

The music is embedded in my consciousness and to me the themes and motifs are like old friends, people of long acquaintance.

No theme ever sounds exactly the same; it is different each time in 'shape' or tempo and as it swirls through my head, I say: 'Ah, here comes old so-and-so'. Of course, I love other music too . . . even some 'pops'! Let that almost forgotten old poet, Lord Tennyson, have the last word:

> There is sweet music here that softer falls
> than petals from blown roses on the grass.
> Or night dew on the still waters between
> walls of shadowy granite, in a gleaming
> pass. Music that gentler on the spirit lies
> Than tired eyelids upon tired eyes.

CHAPTER 59

Some Thoughts About Music

Music is the supreme vehicle of Man's emotions and the song and dance are its earliest manifestations. The joy of life and our consciousness of the Divine are instinctively felt and expressed in the rhythmic motions of the body, or in the sweet eloquence of the song. Indeed, the song and the dance form the basis of all music and their influence may be traced in the most elaborate orchestral work.

The gradual expansion of the human intelligence provided the necessary stimulus to seek less monotonous means of rhythmic and melodic expression. Thus men sought to obviate the monotony of vocal and instrumental repetition by introducing an element of variety. They discovered, for example, that the same fragment of melody played over and over again was rather a strain on the nervous system. Thus they learned to contrast one melody with another so that interest could be sustained. Any minuet or simple little piece illustrates this. In short, what we 'moderns' understand as 'form' in music resulted from humanity's very natural dislike of being bored!

The same impulse for fuller expression drove men to invent new instruments, and these enabled composers to introduce a new element of 'colour' into their works by exploiting the tonal qualities of these new instruments.

It is hoped that these very sketchy remarks may help us to understand how much we owe to our distant ancestors for their laborious experiments, bequeathed from one generation to another, which made possible the music of the Masters.

CHAPTER 60

O Ye Poor Abandoned Sons and Daughters of Eve! (Start of a Musical Journey)

If you were born in the late fifties and after, you missed, by scarcely a
decade, the glorious epoch of Hollywood glamour and romance and the
flood of songs which came out of Tin Pan Alley in New York and London.
Ah yes, and the stream of great musicals emanating from the theatreland of
London and New York.

Do not despair! All is far from lost, for these treasures have survived
today's feckless fashions and you can still find them by careful research in
any good record shop.

May I invite you to accompany me on a magical adventure, a journey
through the wonderland of recorded music? The period concerned starts
with the year 1912 and runs up to the present day.

Let us begin with the so called 'standards', songs that pass easily from one
decade to the next. These were the songs that the public took to their
hearts. Clever and meaningful lyrics are married to fine – sometimes utterly
beguiling – melodies.

Examine the compilations of Bing Crosby, Frank Sinatra, Johnny Mathis,
Nat 'King' Cole, Matt Munroe, the great Ella Fitzgerald and inimitable 'Fats'
Waller; all these singers recorded many 'standards'.

Another prime source is the dance bands of America and Britain. To
reclaim the earlier standards starting around 1925, a rich source would be
the early dance bands of:

Carroll Gibbons' Savoy Orpheans
The Boston Orchestra (Relief band for the Orpheans)
New Mayfair Dance Orchestra, Ray Noble (with the English Crosby,
    Al. Bowly, a Greek!)
Leslie Jeffries and The Palm Court Orchestra
Albert Sandler and his Palm Court Orchestra (Albert Sandler was a
    virtuoso violinist, famous in classical as well as light music. Leslie Jeffries
    was a superb violinist.)
The famous Palm Court Orchestra was based at The Grand Hotel,
    Eastbourne – in the 30's, a mecca for light music fans.

Then we have the following:-

Billy Cotton	Victor Sylvester (Strict Tempo)	
Roy Fox	Ambrose	Jay Wilbur
Jack Hylton	Jack Payne	Geraldo
Henry Hall	Debroy Somers	Joe Loss

The great American bands were those of:-

Glenn Miller	Duke Ellington	Count Basie
Tommy Dorsey	Russ Morgan	Si Zentner
Woody Herman	Paul Whiteman	Jimmy Dorsey
Benny Goodman	Lionel Hampton	Charlie Barnet
Artie Shaw	Stan Kenton	

I have a feeling that I may have left a top band out of this list. You may blame an old man's memory for that!

The bands cover a wide variety of styles, but those grand old songs are worth a hearing, regardless of style.

CHAPTER 61

Hollywood Films

Another source of fine standards is, of course, the Hollywood films of those golden days.

Let us continue our journey by remembering *Gold Diggers* of 1933, 'We're in the Money'; from *Dames* came, 'I only have eyes for you' (Dick Powell and Ruby Keeler). Again from *Gold Diggers*, 1933 we have 'The Shadow Waltz' and, from *Gold Diggers*, 1935, that lovely song, 'Lullaby of Broadway'.

Who can forget Fred Astaire and Ginger Rogers dancing in films that gave us songs, unique in both lyrics and melodies, listed below?

'Top Hat, White Tie and Tails', 'I'm putting all my eggs in one basket', 'Cheek to Cheek', 'The way you look tonight', 'Pick yourself up', 'Isn't this a lovely day to get caught in the rain?', 'Smoke gets in your eyes', 'They can't take that away from me', 'Let's face the music and dance', 'The Continental', 'A Fine Romance', 'Night and Day'.

America's great composers gave us these songs, Irving Berlin, Jerome Kern/Dorothy Fields, George and Ira Gershwin and Cole Porter.

It is now time to mention the film and theatre musical productions, which have enriched so many lives.

In this short survey of film songs, I believe the following to be of first importance, for they were vehicles of unforgettable cinematic and musical excellence.

Some of these musicals were also significant stage shows.

Oscar Hammerstein II's *Carmen Jones*, a story set to the music of the original score of Bizet's *Carmen*. Starring Dorothy Dandridge and Harry Delafonte, it is the most perfect musical play and deserves a place in the collection of any serious musicals fan.

The incomparable Jeanette MacDonald starred in classic musicals such as 'Desert Song', 'San Francisco', 'Rose Marie', 'Naughty Marietta', 'Maytime', 'Monte Carlo' and, amongst others, 'The Vagabond King'. If we listen to her singing, for example, of 'One alone', from *Maytime*, 'Ah! Sweet Mystery of Life' from *Naughty Marietta*, 'Only a Rose' from *The Vagabond King*, or 'Beyond the Blue Horizon' from *Monte Carlo*, we know we are in the presence of a true diva of screen and stage.

On our journey through the great musicals of stage and screen, it is time to salute the prodigious talent of Rodgers and Hammerstein. Their first successes were *Oklahoma* and *Carousel*, which were soon followed by *The King and I, South Pacific* and *Me and Juliet*. With these wonderful comedies set to gloriously melodious scores, they laid the foundations for the future development of this genre.

The King and I, originally with Yul Brynner and Gertrude Lawrence, brought the mysterious Orient in ravishing costume and stage effects.

The King and I is perhaps the greatest play from a theatrical point of view, for it avoids the pleasant flipperies of most musicals and in its libretto blends elements of high drama with elegant comedy. The conflict between the strait-laced but beautiful teacher from the West and the primitive, but fascinating, Oriental monarch makes for fine theatre and was given a magical score.

Fast and furious rustic love and comedy made *Oklahoma* immortal. The score is studded with unforgettable songs; who could forget 'Oh what a beautiful morning', 'The surrey with the fringe on top', 'Out of my dreams', 'People will say we're in love'? Such songs were the perfect showcase for singers of the calibre of Howard Keel and Enzio Pinza.

Another rollicking Western-style musical to raise a storm of acclamation all over the world is *Annie Get Your Gun*. Betty Hutton's explosive talent carries us along at a furious pace in 'Doin' what comes naturally' and 'I got the sun in the morning' and her duets with that splendid singer Howard Keel become permanent fixtures, once heard, in the memories of countless fans. Howard Keel's solos are pure delight as he renders those spanking tunes 'The girl that I marry' and 'My defences are down'. The comedy duet with Betty Hutton, 'Anything you can do' and 'They say it's wonderful'. The last-named comedy duet is fine melody wedded to a genuinely witty comedy lyric. A joy to the ear!

Irving Berlin's sparkling score contains 'There's no business like show business', which is now the anthem of the entire entertainment industry.

This is but one of MGM contributions to musicals. The imperatives of time and space preclude a detailed description of all.

Not merely for patriotic reasons do I list first some early British musicals, which, by virtue of their Englishness, have in this age all but disappeared from the public mind.

No, No, Nanette was first performed at the Palace Theatre on London's Shaftsbury Avenue on March 11th 1925. Oddly enough, it had already proved a success in Detroit. The score by Vincent Youmans contains a song of universal appeal even today, 'Tea for Two'.

The Buccaneer. This musical play with lyrics and music by Sandy Wilson was first performed at a London Club theatre in 1953. It is not a story about piracy on the high seas, but a love story woven around a boys' magazine and its struggle to survive against rival American comics. The whole atmosphere of this charming piece of musical theatre is firmly rooted in the twenties, a time when schoolboys eagerly awaited their weekly comics and magazines. I find it all very nostalgic for I too read *Gem*, *Boys Own Paper*, *The Wizard* and *The Magnet*. It deserves a worthy place in any serious collection of musicals.

The Boyfriend. Again with lyrics and music by Sandy Wilson, this is another precious memento of the so-called roaring twenties.

First given in its full score at the Players Theatre in October 1953, it was originally planned to run for three weeks, but that first performance so delighted the audience that the play was transferred to the Embassy Theatre for the Christmas Season. It is a strange fact that many London Theatre managements turned down this musical as 'not commercial'. Later there came a flood of offers and the successful bidder was Sir Bronson Albury, owner of the Wyndham Theatre, where it enjoyed one of London's longest runs.

The Boyfriend vividly evokes a period of our recent history with its charming words and music. It breathes the very atmosphere of a Britain, of an England, that has slipped away into the mists of time.

The Water Gypsies. This musical play was the result of a happy meeting of minds and music between gifted British composer Vivian Ellis and distinguished man of letters, A.P. Herbert. Based on a famous book called *The Water Gypsies*, it has a very unusual backdrop, for it must have been difficult to make a successful stage production out of a story about the River Thames tideway and canals.

The storyline is a complex one, but these two talented gentlemen swept all such objections aside and produced a British winner at a time when the London theatres were full of major American shows. Serious collectors will not pass it by.

Wild Grows the Heather is a musical inspired by the late Sir John Barrie's novel, *The Little Minister*. Set in the little Scottish town of Thrums in the reign of King George IV, it tells of a weavers' revolt against the King's representative, the Earl of Rintoul. The Redcoats arrive and their Captain discusses with the Earl plans to arrest the ringleaders. However, their plans are betrayed to the weavers by the Earl's lovely daughter, who, disguised as a gypsy, meets the Minister for Thrums in a wood and persuades him to blow three times on a horn, a secret warning to the weavers that the Redcoats are coming. Babbie, as the Earl's daughter is known, is herself hunted by the soldiers, but eludes them in disguise. Then love enters the story. The Minister falls madly and hopelessly in love with Babbie and the Kirk elders are so enraged by the Minister's infatuation that they eject him from his manse and from the Kirk.

The Minister goes to Rintoul to plead for the release of the gipsy, since arrested by the soldiers. At the castle he is astonished to meet his 'gipsy', now in her true position as the daughter of the Earl. Angry at her deception, he departs. The Lady Barbara, once the gipsy girl, tells her father that she means to marry the Minister. The Earl intends to prevent the marriage of his only daughter to a poor Minister but all is well that ends well, for the lovers defy the Earl and marry.

All the Scottish romantic drama is embraced in delightful music and this musical shares with another Scottish musical, *Brigadoon*, the robust atmosphere of the Scottish heather and the spirit of this ancient people.

A major British contributor to the stage and film musical art-form is Lionel Bart. His *Oliver*, skilfully adapted from the Dickens novel, keeps close to the story and dresses key situations in original songs, each one memorable, not just for the tunes, but also for the lyrics.

Nancy's love song, 'As long as he needs me', tears your heart out. The orphan boys' dining room scene, so poignant in the novel, is transferred into hilarity as the boys sing 'Food glorious food'. Crafty old Fagin, in 'Reviewing the situation', attains poetic comedy and 'You've got to pick a pocket or two' proves irresistible to the urchins under his charge. On stage and in the film, this is a wonderful creation, and one that will hold its place indefinitely in public affection. A film and stage classic, it can stand side by side with the greatest American achievements in this art form.

America's film giant, MGM, has made a massive contribution to the treasury of major musicals. Some are legends, absolutely and permanently locked in to the lives of worldwide audiences.

Especially for any very young readers, let me have the inestimable privilege of drawing your attention to some musicals which, if you are unaware of them today, may yet enrich your life if only you can seek them out in your record store.

Can Can music by Cole Porter evokes the bohemian gaiety of Paris with show-stopping tunes such as 'C'est magnifique', 'Allez-vous en', 'I love Paris' and the rip-roaring 'Can Can'.

Show Boat. The sound-track of this film is superb. In it star Howard Keel, a giant among the many gifted male artists featured in musicals, lovely Kathryn Grayson and that mysterious, ever-fascinating actress, Ava Gardner.

The songs in this musical are now part of American folklore.

'Can't help lovin' dat man', 'I still suits me', 'Make Believe', 'Ol' man River', 'Why do I love you?' are sung in bath tubs all over the world, especially 'Ol' man river', immortalised by that glorious bass, Paul Robeson. The comedy duet sung by Paul Robeson and Elizabeth Welch, 'I still suits me', allows these two fine artists to enjoy themselves with Paul Robeson as a lazy good-for-nothing husband who uses all the umbrella and leaves all the housework to his long-suffering wife. She, in spite of everything, loves him still.

On stage and screen Jerome Kern's score and the artists associated with it have made *Show Boat* a musical that will endure ad infinitum.

Another successful MGM film soundtrack featured Fred Astaire, Jack Buchanan and Nanette Fabray. *Bandwagon* had a generous share of the best songs of that time and some survive today: 'You and the night and the music', 'Dancing in the dark', 'I guess I'll have to change my plan', 'Something to remember you by', 'A shine on your shoes' and the exciting 'Louisiana Hayride'.

MGM's *American in Paris*, with a song-studded score by George and Ira Gershwin, was received with rapture by audiences captivated not only by the storyline set in Paris with all the romantic overtones of that lovely city. It bewitched them with songs of pure delight. Gene Kelly, multi-talented singer and dancer, was the perfect partner for beautiful waif-like Lesley Caron.

Who can forget those delightful children sharing 'I got rhythm'. They broke up the first line with an infectious humour to which the inimitable Gene Kelly replied 'rhythm'. There followed 'Embraceable you', ''S wonderful', 'Tra la la', the indescribable 'Our love is here to stay' and 'Stairway to paradise'.

This is one of the truly great musicals, for it combines Gallic romance with American show business and it does so within a musical framework unique in rhythmic and melodic appeal; it is a 'must' for every serious collector.

It is time to take our leave of the MGM musicals and to close this section by hoping that some readers may be enticed to seek them out in their record shops.

I believe musicals are dying, for who can expect melody, fine lyrics and romantic story lines from a society like ours at this period in our history? Materially we are very rich. Even the poor, compared with millions in Asia, Africa and South America, are assured of a survival income. Moreover it is a sex-obsessed society which spurns true love and uses ugly, demeaning phrases like 'having sex' and 'partner'.

Can you name a truly significant musical written since the 70's? Can you, dear reader, with hand on heart, name one film or a single beautiful production on the New York or London stage? The last great durable musicals were:-

My Fair Lady – Fiddler On The Roof – Gigi

My Fair Lady is musical theatre *par excellence*. Everything about it is absolutely perfect. The story of the cockney girl and the university professor, who transforms this ignorant daughter of a common coster father into a beautiful high society lady, is superb theatre; the casting too, faultless. Wilfred Hyde White, as the prototype English gentleman, acts as a superb foil to high-handed Professor Higgins. And, then there is the pert and pretty Eliza Dolittle, who treats the professor with bewitching impertinence. Audrey Hepburn's performance is pure enchantment. The imperious Professor Higgins is brought to book by the cockney flower girl from London's Covent Garden. She marries him! Eliza's costermonger dad in a whirlwind dance, ensures that he 'Gets to the church on time!' Rex Harrison the Professor, Audrey Hepburn as Eliza and Stanley Holloway as Eliza's father carry this wonderful musical with splendid élan.

And then, the songs, 'I could have danced all night', 'On the street where you live', 'You did it!', 'The rain in Spain', 'Without you', 'With a little bit of luck', 'I've grown accustomed to her face', 'I'm an ordinary man' and 'Wouldn't it be lovely!'

What a script, what a story, what songs, what stars! *My Fair Lady* has everything; it is a masterpiece of musical theatre and film. A fine supporting cast includes veteran actress Gladys Cooper. Based on Bernard Shaw's *Pygmalion*, the lyrics were by Alan Jay Lerner and the music was composed by Frederick Loewe.

Fiddler on The Roof, set in a small Russian village around the beginning of the last century, is the tale of a man, his family and his relations with his fellow citizens in good times and bad.

This musical defies all cultural, racial and religious barriers and its message is universal. Whilst the theme is profoundly religious, this is a joyous musical, yet reflecting the oppression and social problems of its period. Above all, it stresses the truth that belief in God is the only sure basis for a safe, decent and caring society. The life of the inhabitants of that village, Anatevka, is rooted in this basic principle. It is brought to light only through ancient and precious traditions, which were under attack in those far-off Czarist days, as they are now in the new 21st century. *Fiddler On The*

Roof strenuously defends these old values, which can be summarised by describing the manner and opinions of the village milkman, Tevye. In his village each individual knows his or her responsibilities. Each knows what God wishes him or her to do. Father heads the household and is, by divine right, head of the house. To his wife Tevye shows reverence as spouse and mother. Mother keeps the home and Father struggles with a hard world to maintain it. His daughters have their household duties and, by tradition, have their husbands chosen for them by the matchmaker, whose choices are by no means in accord with those young ladies' wishes.

Tevye, the philosopher milkman, requires his sons to work hard at school and at their trades. He has his place in the community, like the Rabbi and village constable. Each plays his part, just as the village baker, tailor, butcher and schoolmaster do, and Tevye reminds them all that without respect for old traditions, life would be as precarious as a *Fiddler On The Roof.*

The overall message of this hugely successful musical is to impress upon us all that, flowing from respect for the Deity, comes order and human love, and that by keeping old traditions, we acquire true happiness.

Let us revert to Tevye and his daughters. Tradition says that Father must approve the marriages arranged by the matchmaker, but this time Tevye rejects that tradition. His love for his daughters compels him to accept *their* choices for husbands. At his eldest daughter's wedding, Tevye, his wife Goldie and friends, toast the happy couple and the local inn resounds to lively singing and dancing. They raise their glasses and sing 'To life, L'chaim'.

The delighted bridegroom, overflowing with happiness, sings a joyous song, 'Miracle of Miracles'. Tevye's second daughter Hodel and her fiancé express their heartfelt gratitude to Tevye for, just once, defying tradition and blessing both marriages.

On stage and on the screen, the wedding ceremony is moving and beautiful – an event celebrated by a candle-lit procession under a golden canopy, in accordance with ancient tradition. Tevye and Goldie share that sad yet joyful moment known to parents at weddings, when they lose a daughter – an event they express in that spellbinding and emotional song, 'Sunrise, Sunset' (A discreet handkerchief might be useful here). At this point in the proceedings, the males who are agile enough perform the bottle dance whilst the young ladies dance a lively ballet. High spirits, good food and music make this a wedding to remember; on stage and screen alike, it is a colourful and invigorating episode.

Around this village the peasants and workers are in revolt. An ugly anti-Semitism, instigated by Czarist ministers, brings these happy celebrations to a halt. Cossacks and angry Russian peasants stream into Anatevka, looting, burning and assaulting villagers. The wedding guests do not escape this cruel and unhappy event. When the situation subsides and some kind of normality returns, Tevye reminds Goldie that whatever happens, the most important thing in life is love. 'Do you', he asks Goldie wistfully, 'love me?' She answers, 'I suppose I do'; a lovely song follows at this point.

More than 35,000,000 people have seen and heard *Fiddler On The Roof*, on stage or in film in more than 32 countries. The première was given in New York during September 1964.

A glorious bonus on the sound track of the original motion picture is the presence of international violin virtuoso, Isaac Stern, whose superlative playing enchants and adds lustre to one of the historic musicals of all time. The violin is exactly the right voice to tell this story and this violinist is a truly inspired 'narrator'. The opening prologue and melody 'Tradition' features Mr Stern with Tevye, chorus and orchestra. There follows 'Matchmaker', and soon after that, the showstopper song sung by Tevye, 'If I were a rich man'. There are so many jewels in this score: 'Sabbath prayer' with Tevye, Goldie and Isaac Stern chorus and orchestra, 'To life', and 'Miracle of miracles'.

A supreme moment comes with 'Sunrise, Sunset' sung by Tevye, Goldie, Perchik and daughter Hodel. The finale is grand indeed, with the magic bow of Isaac Stern and the orchestra.

That magnificent Israeli actor and singer, Topol takes the part of Tevye. His wife Goldie is most movingly portrayed by Norma Crane. And a most gifted cast includes . . . our own Ruth Madoc as Fruma Sarah.

This is no mere musical. It is also a social document, whose essential message is valid today in every country on earth. It fiercely, yet with marvellous music, lays down a code of conduct for all mankind.

Our last port of call before leaving the magical land of musicals is to Gigi. The music is by Frederick Loewe and the libretto by Alan Jay Lerner; it is another masterpiece by those superbly talented men who gave us *My Fair Lady* – a most happy co-operation.

This musical is about Paris and about Frenchmen. Is there an Anglo-Saxon male who, in his secret heart, would not give up football, beer and cricket in exchange for that (for women!) mesmerising Latin charm, that accent, that peculiarly Gallic gesture involving both hands and facial expression? Monsieur Maurice Chevalier embodies all that. In the 30's there was not a woman in Europe who could resist that legendary Frenchman, who first won the hearts of British women in that lovely film, *Innocents of Paris*. That smile, that shrug of the shoulders, and we Englishmen must slink away and drown ourselves in envy.

This film also provides a guided tour of Paris, with lovely shots of M. Chevalier and the delightful Gigi driving through the Bois de Bologne on a sunny afternoon.

How pert, how pretty the delectable Leslie Caron is as Gigi. When Maurice sings 'Thank heaven for little girls, for little girls get bigger every day,' you can tell he means it!

Directed by Vincent Minelli, the magnificent cast included one of those legendary Hungarian Hollywood sisters, Eva Gabor, as well as Louis Jordan, the celebrated Hermione Gingold, Isobel Jeans, and Jacques Bergerac. If the year 1948 is to be remembered for anything, it should be as the year that gave to the world adorable *Gigi* and Paris. *Gigi's* attractive score contains the lovely *Gigi* theme, 'The night they invented champagne', the song of an old fellow who still has an eye for a pretty girl. 'Thank heaven for little girls' needs no further praise, and neither does that charming humorous exchange between Maurice Chevalier and his lady when, lost in nostalgia, she recalls the early days of love and he gets the facts wrong: 'I remember it well'.

Paris! The trees in the Bois de Boulogne seem to whisper words of love in the breeze. The Olympia and Maxim's music halls, the street cafés and the Moulin Rouge make this city the mecca of hedonists. It is the modern Elysium. *L'Amour toujours l'amour.* This musical is a celebration of a city and of Gallic romance – utterly delightful.

Oh ye sons and daughters born in the late 50's and after, you are our tomorrow and you can claw back those lost treasures in music. If I have been granted the privilege of awakening your interest, you can enjoy yourselves researching the music of yesterday by tracking them down in your local record stores. Happy hunting!

CHAPTER 62

Obituary (For the Musical)

It all began back in the twenties with Al Jolson singing 'Mammy' in *The Jazz Singer*. There followed the endearing Eddy Cantor in *Roman Scandals*, singing that catchy little song 'We'll build a little home'. Then came the Broadway Melodies of 1933 and 1935, the advent of the 'talkies', which set the wheels in motion that carried us forward to so many great films and shows. There will be no more great romantic films or shows, for we live now in a society where romance is mocked and not understood. How can an age cursed with material plenty, but at the same time with spiritual poverty, create anything beautiful? We now have the drug culture, the deliberate efforts by powerful people to downgrade marriage and the family. An age where those ugly words 'partner' and 'having sex' prevail is moribund. Who could write a lovely tune, for instance, such as 'Ah! Sweet mystery of life at last I've found you' in a squalid era, sex-obsessed and deprived of true romance based on mutual reverence between men and women?

Today flouts the past. I feel sad that most of those gifted artists and composers who created the musical as an art form are now, as sailors say, 'In Davy Jones' locker' – dead!

But, I must not be too sad, for most people today are kind and decent, even though exposed to dreadful influences; the good have lost control. Perhaps the pendulum of history will swing back and we may yet see a world that can create great productions for stage and screen with glorious music and artists to perform it.

Young ones, it is up to you! But hurry... it may already be too late.

CHAPTER 63

The Great Tenors

The recording sessions made by Enrico Caruso in Milan in 1902 are of enormous significance, for not only did they launch this phenomenal artist on his international career, they also laid the historical foundations of the record industry.

Instead of being a novelty, a kind of amusing toy, Caruso's Milan sessions established the newly arrived wind-up gramophone as a wholly credible vehicle for musical performances on wax.

Thus was opened epoch of the great recording industry. In the following decades a procession of illustrious singers emerged whose performances in Grand Opera, classical *Lieder*, Viennese operetta and great stage and film performances were to enthral the world.

In all this the tenor voice was supreme and Caruso's successors were legion. Perhaps it will be both interesting and helpful if I name the most eminent. In some cases I will mention a particular record inseparable from a famous tenor.

E. Caruso (Died 1921)	*Vesti la giubba*	Pagliacci (Leoncavallo)
Tito Chipa	*Una furtive lagrima*	L'elisir d'amore (Donizetti)
B. Gigli (Died 1957)	*Che gelida manina*	La Bohème (Puccine)
R. Tauber (Died 1948)	*You are my heart's delight*	Land of Smiles (F. Lehar)
J. McCormack (Died 1945)	*Bless this house* (and all the great Irish standards)	(Brahé)
Jussi Bjorling (Died 1960)	*Nessun dorma*	Turandot (Puccini)
Heddle Nash (Died 1961)	*Dream song*	Manon (Massenet)

Perhaps the only major international tenor of English nationality was Heddle Nash. He was called 'the English Bjorling'.

Two important examples of the art of the earlier great tenors are the

136

German tenors, Marcel Wittrisch and Helga Roswaenge. We should also include one enormously gifted Frenchman, Georges Thill.

There is a legion of tenors, too many to detail here, but lovers of the tenor voice can track them down in record stores. Each one has rich treasures to offer you if you dare to seek them out.

I list some below:-

Charles Kullman	Nicolai Gedda	Hans Hopf
Richard Lewis	Richard Crooks	David Lloyd
F. Tagliavini	G. Di Stefano	Walter Widdop
L. Melchior	F. De Lucia	G. Martinelli
Lee Slezak	H. Ernst Groh	Peter Schreier
Peter Dawson		

Tenors come in different styles. Those called 'light' tenors specialise in operetta or Neapolitan songs. Some interpret the rich heritage of German classic songs, the celebrated 'Lieder' of F Schubert and Hugo Wolf, who wrote beautiful settings for the poet Goethe. He drew on mainly literary sources, which were grouped as Italian and Spanish 'Lieder' (Song) books.

Other tenors express romantic passion and for a classic example of this style, I commend a newcomer to Opera seria to listen to: G. Di Stefano's ardent declaration of love for Mimi in the aria 'Che gelida manina', 'Your tiny hand is frozen', which reaches a climatic declaration of romantic passion in the heavenly duo with Maria Callas, 'O soave fanciulla'. It achieves an emotional intensity, breathtaking in its attack on our senses. Such fire, and such red-blooded desire to love and be loved, makes this utterly unforgettable.

The repertoire of tenors is very large and it would be impossible here to list them all. But with a little research, dear readers, you can enrich your lives. However, lady readers beware! Every tenor aria, every tenor song, serious or gay, is a cupid's dart aimed right at your heart!

Great Ladies of Music on Discs

Dame Nellie Melba and Scandinavian's divine Jenny Lind were, I believe, the first great divas of the vocal art. The last-named legendary Swedish soprano died in 1887, just before the advent of the recorded voice. She settled in Britain and became a revered teacher at the Royal College of Music. It is written that her voice had a haunting beauty never to be forgotten by those who heard her sing.

Australian born diva, Dame Melba, laid the foundation stone for the record-pressing factory of The Gramophone Company (later EMI) at Hayes, Middlesex.

Many other famous ladies were to follow and because of their place in the history of recorded music, I name some of them below. Most can still be found in specialist record shops.

Elizabeth Schuman	Elizabeth Schwarzkopf	Joan Sutherland
Lucia Popp	Elsie Morrison	Clara Ebers
Emmy Bettendorf	Janet Baker	Montserat Baballe
Victoria de Los Angeles	Gallia-Curci	Geraldine Farrar
Licia Albanese	Erna Berger	Emma Calve
Kirsten Flagstad	Tiana Lemnitz	Lily Pons
Maria Caniglia	Rosa Ponselle	Luisa Tetrazzini
Sena Jurinac		

Two particular famous recordings will make you fight back your tears as you listen to them. They are of renderings by two of the most superb contraltos of our, or any other, time. The first is 'I have lost my Euridice' from *Orfeo ed Euridice* by C.W. Gluck, sung by the late Kathleen Ferrier. The second is 'Softly awakes my heart' from *Samson et Dalila* by Saint-Saens, sung ineffably by Marion Anderson. Finally we must include the truly divine Maria Callas.

We have reached the end of our musical journey. I hope my readers may find something of interest that will spur them on to discover new delights. For my omissions, misspellings or other errors, I ask their indulgence. Music, the only truly international language, is the gift bestowed upon us that can unite all humanity. Together these wondrous talents proclaim that one day '. . . All men shall be brothers'. Music of all kinds brings that happy day, yet so distant, nearer.

CHAPTER 64

The Light Orchestral Repertoire

In between classical symphonic and popular dance music lies a rich field of light music of a semi-classical form, with a host of lovely melodies dressed in beautiful orchestral tone colours.

Below is a list of some of the most popular, with a mention of some of the orchestras associated with this type of music.

Andrew Kostalanetz	George Melachrino
Mantovani	Paul Whiteman
Maurice Winnick	David Rose
Ray Noble	Al Goodman
Frank Cordell	Marek Weber
Jack Hylton	New Light Symphony
James Last	Phil Green
Ron Goodwin	Mayfair
London Palladium	Tommy Dorsey
Ray Anthony	Glen Miller
Duke Ellington	Vaughn Monroe
Percy Faith	Norrie Paramour
Ray Martin	Franck Pourcel
Ambrose	Wal-Berg
Artie Shaw	Jack Payne
Joe Loss	Geraldo
Victor Silvester	Count Basie
Roy Fox	Henry Hall
Ray Ventura	

It will not be easy to track some of these fine orchestras, for the Rock revolution has pushed them aside in the changing fashions of our time. But, some can still be rescued from obscurity either in private collections or, in a few cases, they can be resurrected by means of the CD disc.

Sweet music, it used to be called, but this lovely repertoire is not insipid or saccharine. It allows modern orchestras, manned by top-class musicians, to display their talent and show the orchestra in all its splendour.

CHAPTER 65

Those Were the Days.
Two Historic Records

Another historic record for the collector interested in British radio
successes from the past is this recording of favourite radio themes. The
programme begins with the sound of Bow Bells and Oranges and Lemons,
an item from *Housewives Choice*. This is followed by a dance band medley
featuring Joe Loss, Jack Payne's opening theme *Say it with Music* and various
much loved items from *Dick Barton, Special Agent, Variety Band Box, Music
While You Work* (much enjoyed by factory workers during World War II),
Workers' Playtime and *Billy Cotton Band Show*.

Side Two of this treasure from our British past contains the Greenwich
time signal, *Two-Way Family Favourites*, a comedy medley with *Hancock's
Half Hour*, Ted Ray in *Ray's a Laugh, Mrs Dale's Diary, The Archers* and *Henry
Hall's Guest Night*, ending with his farewell tune, 'Here's to the next Time'.

A rare nostalgic treat for the over-fifties and worth a hearing by the
younger listeners to give them an idea of what radio was like in the pre-
Beatles era.

The music on this record is by Paul Fenoulhet and the *London Concert
Orchestra* with a very popular vocal group of those days, *The Star Gazers*.

Announcements are by one of the BBCs most popular radio announcers,
Alvar Lidell.

Famous voices and dearly loved melodies make this a truly indispensable
item for collectors who care about those not-so-far-away times, which may
justly be called the golden age of British Radio.

This record was issued by *United Artists Records* under the title *Those Were
The Days*. The record number is UAG 29739.

Postscript: The Sounds of Time

(Oriole MG-20021) A Dramatisation of the Years 1934 to 1949

For readers interested in recent dramatic history, this rare record contains
the voices of the following who played a key role in those earth-shaking
events.

Sir Winston Churchill
Princess Elizabeth
General Eisenhauer
A. Hitler
S. Baldwin
R. Weizmann
J.B. Priestley
E. Bevin

King George VI
C. Atlee
H.G. Wells
B. Mussolini
P. Nehru
W. Joyce (Haw-Haw)
King George V
President Truman

President Roosevelt
F.M. Montgomery
Sir N. Chamberlain
R. MacDonald
Tommy Handley
General De Gaulle
H. Goering
Duke of Edinburgh

Events covered by this precious record are:

Arnhem, The London Blitz, Royal Wedding, Rhine Crossing, Abdication Speech, Hindenburg Disaster, The Liberation of Paris, El Alamein, The Battle of Britain, The Victory Celebration. Released by that valiant little British record company, *Oriole* in association with the BBC.

PART V

Personalities

CHAPTER 66

The Finzals

The Finzal family consisted of parents and twin sons, John and James. In the 20's and 30's they lived at 342 Brixton Road in South London. Their house was a large three-storey building with a square roof, having a surround of paving stones just like those in the road below, so that one could walk around the perimeter with relative safety. The significance of all this will become clear as my story unfolds.

John and James, like their parents, were highly intelligent and fluent in French and German. It was a very cultured family. At the time my young brother Billy and I knew them, they were 'teenagers' and we were both rather younger. I was about ten and Billy six.

The twins had drawn poor cards in the lottery of life. They attended a famous South London school and, on the academic side, were brilliant. They were extremely effeminate and walked with the same gait as young women. This was the cause of much teasing on the part of Billy and me. We knew it not, but they were homosexuals. John and James had high-pitched voices and, alike as two pins, were natural comedians with a huge sense of fun.

John used to tell us that he was madly in love with a boy in his form named Berman. 'I am going to marry Berman and have my honeymoon in the (newly opened) Brixton Astoria.'

Billy and I used to play a dangerous game with John. We would call out, 'Berman hates you,' or 'Berman despises you,' and John, his face distorted with rage, would rush at us wielding a tennis racquet or whatever weapon was to hand. Then, just a moment or so before he could reach us, we would quickly shout, 'No, he adores you, he worships you!' and John's face would undergo a rapid transformation and assume a beatific smile. Then he would glow with sheer delight. You had to get the timing right. By using our Berman power, we could make John our slave to do our bidding.

It was, I believe, about 1929 when the Brixton Astoria opened, a beautiful luxury cinema with artificial blue sky and stars. There were two films with a splendid stage show interpolated between. I remember Jack Hylton's band and the brilliant xylophone player, Teddy Brown, and many more class acts. Value for money in those days! The usherettes were divinely pretty in Cambridge Blue suits with cream blouses. We boys used to occupy the cheapest seat (sixpence, I believe), and then crawl under the seats to arrive eventually at the two-and-threepenny seats. Often we were caught and returned to the front row.

The seats were plush-covered and lovers used to sit in the rear ones and enjoy a cuddle whilst watching the latest Hollywood epic. Today the Astoria, renamed 'Brixton Academy' (some academy!), is a dump. On that opening day the first thousand were let in free. Yes, Billy and I were there!

James, although as eccentric as his brother, expressed his strange personality differently. Both boys were tall, slender and endowed with frail physiques, both as alike as two pins. Their sallow complexions were crowned with jet back hair and their eyes could sparkle like diamonds when they were excited. They looked highly peculiar.

James, often detailed by his mother to go shopping at Cullens, a little way down the Brixton Road, used to take three steps forward and two backwards muttering strange incantations and wildly swinging his basket. As a result of his dawdling gait, he took a long time to complete his journey.

James was a tennis fanatic and the Finzals had a large garden, which, in the summer, used to have a full-sized net stretched across it. He told us he was the French woman's champion, Mademoiselle Suzanne Lenglen, and in games with his brother, used to cavort in their garden court just like a female player, with wild swipes and screeches, imitating the centre-court antics of his idol.

One Saturday afternoon we saw a small crowd standing on the pavement outside 342. We heard a portable gramophone playing Can-Can music and saw the twins dancing on the roof parapet doing a 'Moulin Rouge' chorus routine with arms linked and performing high kicks, to the great delight of the crowd. But, we wondered, would they lose their balance and fall from the rooftop to the ground? Mercifully they did not and after much applause from below, they vanished.

One day, feeling safe in the garden of 338, two gardens away from the Finzals, I shouted over the wall, 'Berman loathes you!' A moment later I was struck on the head by a piece of brick cast by an enraged John. The cut bled a little, alarmed my mother and scared the life out of me. In retrospect, I think John was entitled to his revenge.

One enduring memory I have of these very nice, but sad, boys is of the occasion when Billy and I saw them in their military uniforms, issued to them by their school Officer Cadet Corps. 'Dance for us,' said mischievous Billy, and they did their chorus-girl high-kick routine, which amused two naughty boys enormously.

I hope life was kind to them and wonder whether the War hurt them. I heard years later that John had died. As I went into the Navy, I never saw James or his parents again.

Comedy and tragedy are fused together in the lives of the Finzal boys. I feel sad when I think of them and of our constant teasing. I wish Billy and I could have had more understanding of their predicament in the world.

CHAPTER 67

Theatreland – Ivor Novello

In World War I the theatre sensation was *Chu Chin Chow*. In World War II it was Ivor Novella's *Dancing Years*, a masterpiece of refined and tender romance, with such lovely songs as 'Waltz of my Heart', 'I can give you the Starlight', 'My dearest Dear and Primrose'. It brought the audience to its feet, this *Dancing Years*, which, in 1939, was temporarily silenced at Drury Lane by the onset of World War II.

Young reader, if you do not know this musical play, you will be able to experience genuine romantic sentiment expressed in songs of real beauty.

It made a star of that beautiful singer Roma Beaumont. Mary Ellis, who shared honours with Roma in *Dancing Years*, leapt to stardom after her huge success in Ivor Novello's *Glamorous Night*. At one stage this talented man, who wove a magic spell, had four successive stage musicals in which intensive romantic sentiment fused sometimes with genteel comedy and even on occasion, with moments of drama, and all within a framework of haunting melody.

The Mary Ellis solos and duets with Trefor Jones in *Glamorous Night* brought the Drury Lane Theatre audience to its feet; they reeled out of the theatre with the title melody ringing in their ears and intoxicated by 'Fold your Wings', 'Shine through my Dreams', and 'When the Gipsy played'. They had experienced a night to remember for ever. Nor must we forget those luscious orchestral arrangements, so beautifully played by the Drury Lane Theatre Orchestra under the baton of Charles Prentice . . . Theatre magic *par excellence*.

Ivor Novello's last, and some say, his greatest achievement for the musical theatre was *King's Rhapsody*, in which, most unexpectedly, he wrote a major role for himself. There is no doubt that he dearly loved this musical play, in which the lovely Vanessa Lee had a starring role, as did the very talented Olive Gilbert.

King's Rhapsody opened at The Palace Theatre, London, on the 15th September, 1949 and ran for 839 performances.

Because Ivor Novello's personality was an integral part of the play, there could not be an acceptable successor, so although this musical lives on in

148

our time through the miracle of the disk, CD or tape, it remains his own requiem.

Actor, dramatist and composer, Ivor Novello is England's Franz Lehar. His early death on March 5th 1951 has deprived us of many a song and perhaps several musicals, which will now never be heard. We shall never see his like again.

CHAPTER 68

Sir Noel Coward

There seems to be an affinity of talent between Noel Coward and Ivor Novello. Is it their 'Englishness'?

Yes! Both loved England, both expressed her soul.

Like Ivor Novello, Noel was actor, composer, but perhaps not a dramatist, for Sir Noel cast his English eye over men and things and focused a kindly, but highly civilised, eye on the world. He gently teased our foibles and cast upon us all a benign smile.

If he was not a dramatist, he certainly handled dramatic situations superbly as an actor. Anyone who saw him as the tough but human RN Captain in *In Which we Serve* saw how totally convincing he was as a brave leader who, when his ship sank, found himself covered in oil in the sea with his survivors.

However, the Sir Noel with whom most people feel a bond is the creator of his famous cabaret at the *Café de Paris* singing, 'Someday I'll find you' from *Private Lives*, then, 'Poor little rich girl' from that charming opus redolent of the 20's. That song was a sly dig at the debutantes. One of his biggest successes was 'A Room with a View' from the CB Cochran revue, *This Year of Grace*.

Another memorable song was '*Dearest Love*', the waltz song from *Operette*. His comic muse found full scope in 'Mrs Worthington' and who could escape the tender pathos of 'I'll see you again' from *Bitter Sweet*. Another song that will never be forgotten is 'The Stately Homes of England', a gentle leg-pull at the aristocracy.

How can one leave the subject of Sir Noel without reference to three of his song masterpieces? 'London Pride' was his hymn to the capital, the city he loved in its hour of peril. It has a touching air of melancholy, but is full of a decently restrained patriotism combined with immense dignity. Somehow it made us less afraid – and quietly proud to share London's ordeal during the Blitz.

Some of us can remember his duet with Yvonne Printemps, the sublime 'I'll follow my secret heart', which floods the heart with tender longing.

Finally we have 'Mad Dogs and Englishmen'. We used to hear frequent mention of this satirical comic classic in hot places like Aden or Singapore.

Naval regulations insist that ratings wear their regulation sun helmets in such places and whenever we donned this necessary headgear, we thought of Sir Noel and *Mad Dogs*.

Sir Noel Coward and William Shakespeare were both men of the theatre. How they would have revelled in each other's company!

CHAPTER 69

Roy Rogers, King of the Cowboys

In the late 50's, Roy Rogers and his country singer wife, Dale Evans, visited London on a promotional visit to EMI London, who represented his many recordings for the old Regal Zonophone catalogue.

They were a couple of immense charm and courtesy; a true lady and gentleman of American country style music.

A reception was held for them in the Savoy hotel that media representatives attended.

I took my small son, dressed in full cowboy attire, and Mr Rogers was so gracious as to play cowboys with my Philip; they chased each other firing toy pistols all round the Rogers' suite; Mrs Rogers too was kind and remarked on our son's apple-clear complexion.

The only missing guest was Mr Roger's famous horse, 'Trigger'.

Roy Rogers, the King of the Cowboys, shares a moment with our son
Philip at a Savoy Hotel reception, 1958.

CHAPTER 70

Bing Crosby

One day during the early 1930's I was strolling across the barrack square of the Royal Naval depot HMS *Drake* in Devonport. Suddenly I heard a voice drifting through the evening air from the mess; it was the rich, fruity resonances of the late Mr Bing Crosby. I remember the song he sang so caressingly; it was 'Thanks a Million' and it was a song, one of many, with which he made the girls swoon. It filled my young heart too with romantic feeling that night as I thought of my distant girlfriend far away in London.

How could I have known that one day in the late 1970's I would sit opposite him across a table in the CBS Recording Studios in Whitfield Street London? At the time I was acting as a link between the famous crooner and the German television Company ZDF (2nd German TV) of Frankfurt. They planned to do a show with Mr Crosby and their singing star, Caterina Valente. Alas it came to naught, for although Mr Crosby was keen to co-operate, he was destined to die on the golf course in Spain soon after the meeting with the German TV representatives in London.

Bing Crosby and Frank Sinatra were the musical idols in the popular music of my generation. How lucky we were to have escaped the ugly discords, banal lyrics and rhythmic frenzies of the ghastly 'sixties!

CHAPTER 71

Mischa Elman

This international violin virtuoso was an artist who always stayed at the Savoy when in London.

I was sent to deliver an important musical score to him and Reception informed Mr Elman, who said, 'Send him up please'.

I knocked on his room door and found myself face to face with a legend. A small neat man with a pleasant manner and smile he said, 'Come in'; seated at a piano was a friend and I knew that they had been making music together.

'We are rehearsing Gabriel Faure's sonata for violin and piano', said Mr Elman. To my amazement he then said, 'Would you like to listen?'

I spent nearly an hour whilst those gifted musicians immersed themselves in the great French composer's delightful work.

The next day at the Royal Albert Hall this kind and gifted man played the three greatest violin concertos; the Brahms, the Mendelssohn and, in the second half of the concert, that supreme vehicle for the violin, Beethoven's concerto.

An evening to remember and Mr Elman too lives forever in my memory.

Three major concertos in one night! An artistic and physical *tour de force*!

CHAPTER 72

Sir James Savile

A worthy Knight is Sir James Savile. One hears little these days about his long years of devotion to the poor and afflicted, for whom he has raised huge sums of money and to whom he has given many hours of unpublicised trolley-pushing and nursing assistance in a major northern hospital, St James, Leeds.

As a TV personality and presenter, his long-running *Jim'll Fix It* series won him a large public and brought happiness to a host of members of the public as well as participants. With Sir James what you see is what you get. He has that Yorkshire directness, that blunt manner that tells you what he says is what he means. No sophisticated fudging of opinions or feelings.

But it was as one of the country's élite DJs that I got to know him, and I have amusing recollections of those days.

In the late '50's – or could it have been the early '60's? – MGM Records hosted a river boat party to celebrate the chart success of Miss Connie Francis' historic recording of 'Who's Sorry Now?'

Outward bound for the ancient port of Greenwich, the steamer carried a precious cargo of top DJs, musical press and other American and British music business VIPs.

As I surveyed our illustrious guests, I was surprised and sad to note that, despite a personal invitation, which he had accepted, Jimmy Savile was not on board.

After we had been underway for around twenty minutes, a speedboat overtook us and Jimmy made a perilous leap to join the party. Delayed for some reason, Jimmy, characteristically resourceful, had joined us after all. His exploit 'lit' up the boat and occasioned much hilarity.

Another occasion comes to mind. Our Japanese licensee requested us to show hospitality to the city of Tokyo's top DJ, who had a daily audience even larger than Jimmy Savile's. The Japanese expressed a special desire that their DJ should meet Mr Jimmy Savile. I called Jimmy and gave him their request. 'Bring him along to the studio,' said Jimmy and the next day we presented ourselves at the BBC studio where his show was in full swing.

The young Japanese was a very serious young man with minimal English. When he was introduced to Jimmy he bowed low. I noticed the

155

Sir James Savile, famous BBC personality with Ted Beston, BBC left and the author right.

difference when he was introduced to me; all I got was a nod. Our young Jap chap listened intently as Jimmy presented his records with his inimitable bantering style, but things were to take a dramatic turn!

Yorkshire-style humour is as far removed from the Japanese humour as we are from Mars, so Jimmy, assuming a mock hostility, asked our Japanese the following quirky question: 'Have you come over here to get my job?' said Jimmy. 'Because, if you have, you will be found floating face downward in the River Thames.'

I do not believe that our Tokyo guest really understood what was said, but he was convinced that it was menacing and unpleasant; he failed absolutely to understand it was all a joke.

His face, naturally inclined to the yellowish complexion of that part of the world, turned the sort of colour you would see in a man seasick in a force 10 Gale! I hastened to tell him Mr Savile was making a joke, but to no avail. This young man from the land of the rising sun indicated he wanted to leave, so we made a hurried and undignified exit.

When this photograph was taken, the Press was full of stories about 'Payola', the practice of record companies paying DJ's and producers money for including records in their programmes. Sir James, I hasten to report is holding a large sum – in Monopoly money!

CHAPTER 73

Dame Shirley Bassey

There can be few places in the world where the unique talent of Dame Bassey is not known and admired; she is a legend. Wherever she goes, she leaves a trail of happiness and her fans are legion.

During my time with United Artists Records I was privileged to be a minor part of her entourage and to have seen at first hand her effect on audiences in many cities. Her voice, with its ruby-rich tonal quality, has a remarkably expressive range and she can move from the comic, as in 'Big Spender', to a tender ballad like 'Something', to dramatic furore as in 'The Greatest Performance of My Life'. Or, she evokes the ultimate in sophistication with 'Diamonds are a Girl's Best Friend'. These are just a few examples from her many chart records. Moreover, this lady defies time. I saw her recently on television and I swear she looks as glamorous as she did all those years ago.

I hope she will forgive me if I reminisce a little. Years ago, when the BBC maintained a strictly high moral tone, a popular DJ called Roger Moffat forgot himself and used a bad word over the air. He was exiled to Radio Hallam, which, in those days, was rather akin to being sent to Siberia.

I received a call from Roger asking if I could help him get an interview with Dame Bassey, to which she kindly agreed. 'Tell him to come during the interval', said Dame Bassey, who was giving a concert at a venue in London.

Roger duly presented himself and knocking on Dame Bassey's dressing room door, I said, 'Roger is here, Dame Bassey'. What I did not know was that Dame Bassey, who although she always appears looking and sounding like a million dollars, was having an 'off' day and feeling anything but glamorous. 'Tell him to naff off!' she said. At this time we were working on her latest single; I think it was 'Something'. Roger, who I hoped would keep this record on his play list to cover middle England, was just behind me. 'I suppose you won't play it now,' I said forlornly. 'Of course I will,' he retorted.

Later, when Dame Bassey was feeling better, she hastened to put matters right and instructed me to ask Roger to send her a tape with questions to which she would reply. So Roger got his interview after all.

Dame Shirley Bassey at a party in her honour aboard HMS Belfast.
The United Artists young ladies were 'sailors' for the night!

I remember too the impact she had in Vienna on those tough professional musicians from the light music section of the world-famous Vienna Philharmonic Orchestra, known as the Wiener Symphoniker. Normally not given to frivolity, these world-class musicians were all smiles and I suspect they really enjoyed working with her.

In Paris and Stockholm she exercised the same happy influence and her sense of fun infected everyone.

Always supremely professional, Dame Bassey's recording sessions were usually completed well within the allotted time-spell. Strict Musicians' Union rules control the amount of time allowed for recording. If the artist did not perform well and several 'takes' were needed, that could mean moving into extra studio time and additional costs for the Record Company. Dame Bassey always came into the studio fully rehearsed.

On one occasion, I recall, she almost lost one of her biggest successes. She had completed her recording programme and there was about ten minutes of studio time remaining. Dame Bassey's musical advisor and friend Noel Rogers, a veteran Tin Pan Alley (Denmark Street) music publisher, said: 'Why don't you do that Italian song, *Grandi, Grandi, Grandi*? We have time.' Dame Bassey, at first a little reluctant, said, 'All right, let's do it'.

At the same party Dame Shirley Bassey receives a silver disc for a quarter-of-a-million sales of 'Something'.

It had a brilliant English lyric by Norman Newall, one of Britain's most talented lyricists and recording managers. It was a very big hit as 'Never, Never, Never!'

In Australia, the United States, South America, Scandinavia (where I danced on Dame Bassey's toes at a post-concert party in the Stockholm Sheraton Hotel) and in all the major cities of Europe, Dame Bassey always left people excited, elated and begging for more. From her they got fine singing, glamour and, on many an occasion, a genuine emotional bond with her audience.

Dame Bassey was one of the very few Western artists whose records are released in Russia. At the time of the Cold War, she melted the Russians' hearts and in many a Russian home today Dame Bassey sings for them and lifts their emotions.

One of her biggest successes was 'Does Anybody Miss Me?' Yes! Shirley, Yes! Your public all over the world. And the reason is given in another of your successes, 'Nobody Does it Like Me!'

The swivel of those famous hips, synchronised with a mighty drum-beat, always brings the house down in 'Big Spender!'

CHAPTER 74

Miss Terri Berg

European promotion of the artists and records issued by the major American Record Company, United Artists, was conducted from their offices in Mortimer Street, London, just a few steps away from Oxford Circus and the BBC in Langham Place.

In the European Coordination office I had, as my assistant, a young lady named Terri Berg. She was my right and my left hand for more than six years and played a major part in the high-pressure activities in the office. These involved the continuing procedures used to popularise a stream of new releases. Information had to be passed on to a large number of branches and licensees in all the countries of Western Europe.

When major artists were sent on promotional tours of Europe, our office was a hive of activity, and much detailed planning had to be carried out before the act concerned left America.

Once we had been given start and finishing dates, between which the artists would be available, our first move was to communicate these dates to all our contacts and to liaise with our branches and licensees in contacting concert promoters, TV and Radio stations and the press of those countries able to offer venues.

We compiled press kits with photographs, posters and biographies and sent these out to all our contacts.

As the concert dates came in, we prepared a master itinerary, which was sometimes complicated because venue dates could clash or the distances could be too great to be practical.

When at last the full list of venues, Radio and TV dates was complete, copies were made and sent to all those concerned, and further copies were handed to the principals and musicians on arrival at London Airport.

It was usual for me to travel with the groups and solo artists, and that was when Miss Berg took over in the London office.

She was an incredible young woman, who could grasp the complex details of a large itinerary swiftly and accurately and was always able to answer questions and give help and advice to our artists, their managers, and the musicians.

My wonderful assistant, Miss Terri Berg.

I cannot guarantee it, but I believe she was among the fastest shorthand writers in the capital and her nimble fingers whizzed over the keyboard even though, as sometimes happened, she might be chatting to a female colleague while typing!

I would give her a considerable amount of dictation and – hey presto – almost before you could say Jack Robinson, it would be beautifully typed and the folder laid before my unbelieving eyes.

One day our Managing Director called me in and said, 'Ronnie, I have bad news for you, I'm going to have to steal your Terri because she is the best girl in the office and I need her.' In a state of shock, I crawled back to my office. 'What's the matter?' asked Miss Berg. 'The MD wants to see you,' I replied.

She returned wearing an expression rather like that of Boadicea when preparing for battle with the Romans. She sat at her desk and wrote the following message, which she handed to the Managing Director:

> I BELONG TO R. BELL'S OFFICE.
> I WORK FOR R. BELL.
> I WILL NOT WORK, NOT EVEN FOR
> ONE SECOND, FOR ANYONE ELSE.
> IT'S BELL/BERG OR NOTHING.

Martin Davis, our charming and very professional MD, took his 'defeat' with a smile. 'You win, Ron,' he said.

I hasten to correct a wrong impression! Do not, dear reader, imagine that it was I who was responsible for Miss Berg's ultimatum to the MD. It was the *job*! Miss Berg and I had one of the most interesting and all-absorbing jobs in the entire record Industry.

We made friends in every European country, even with the Russians. A stream of visitors came to see us and I used to notice that although they talked to me, it was Terri that captured their eyes.

Miss Berg's talents were obvious, but top-class secretarial qualifications were not her only asset. She was very beautiful – indeed, positively distracting. Sometimes I found it hard to concentrate! She had lustrous long auburn hair down to her waist, a petite lissom figure that made male heads swivel, and lovely classical features with a complexion like the white marble of a statue of the Madonna. (If you think I am exaggerating, dear reader, see her photograph.)

After she left UA Records, Miss Berg became Head of Promotion at EMI Records. I could not suppress a crafty smile when, invited to see her at her office, I saw her sitting where I might have sat, dictating to another young lady. Truly, women have taken over from us poor males!

I can never forget Terri Berg. She became, at the end of our partnership, my fiercest critic!

CHAPTER 75

Mr Sakamoto from Japan, 1972

Japan lies at the other side of the world and is therefore remote from our lives in the West. Westerners tend to associate this nation with the fearsome Samurai, the Shinto religion, and Hari Kari. These, coupled with the austere and somewhat daunting character of the people, make it difficult for us to form close personal relations and durable friendships with the Japanese. I never imagined I could call a Japanese my true friend but I found one in the person of M. Sakamoto.

Mr Sakamoto came to London from our licensee, Toshiba, in Tokyo. He represented Liberty Records in Japan. I soon found a rapport with him. His smile was an ear-to-ear one and he quickly acclimatised himself to our ways and our sense of humour. An intelligent young man, he proved an effective support for our records in Japan.

'Saki' as I called him for simplicity, stands revealed as a very human and very charming young man from the Land of the Rising Sun. His personality shines out in the following letter, which he sent me on his return to Tokyo:-

Mr. Ronnie Bell,   February 25, 1972
Head of Promoter,
Artist Relations,
Liberty/UA, Records Ltd.,
Mortimer House,
37-41 Mortimer Str.,
London, W.1,
England

Dear Ronnie,

As you know it very well memories come sweeter as time goes by. You gave me a lot of them and I'm totally at a loss how I can express my thanks to you.

Aged songs and that dreamy lady of your acquaintance's daughter at the 'Old Vienna', your profound saying of 'The young staff gets older because of troubles and the old gets younger because of problems in records

164

business', your soft hand which, shaking it, I believed reflecting your personality, your constant greetings of 'Hello' on the street and so on. Recalling many things in London I feel that I have no other way to say 'thank you' but waiting for your arrival at Tokyo.

I have already reported to Mr Atsumi your idea of exchanging our local artists, tying up with some air-line company. Maybe he will take his first step in this autumn. Prior to it he will be writing to you or asking your advices.

With this letter may I ask you or Terry (your brilliant secretary) to disperse the enclosed pictures.

Finally please give my best regards to Terry. It will be my pleasure to help her in Tokyo if she should make her honey-moon trip to this orient land.

Again, waiting for your visit of our office, I remain.

Yours sincerely,

M Sakamoto

Liberty Department

Note: The 'Old Vienna' was a popular Austrian restaurant in London's Bond Street.

PART VI

Travel

CHAPTER 76

Mel Tormé and Paddy

In Dublin I found myself drinking Guinness with the chauffeur engaged to convey the American singer Mel Tormé and his party to concert venues in the Republic and in Ulster. He was a comical character, with that typical Irish face which combines mirth with menace. If all goes well it is mirth, but say the wrong thing and the menacing aspect of the Irish character comes to the fore. There was a buzz of conviviality in the tavern and I said to – let us call him Paddy – 'Promise not to kill me and I will tell you an Irish joke.' 'If I don't laugh, you'll buy the next round,' he replied. Here, then, comes the joke.

'Did you ever hear about the Irishman who could not understand why his sister had three brothers while he only had two?', I asked Paddy. 'I'll get the next round', he said when he stopped laughing. Thus encouraged, I went on: 'Would you like another joke, Paddy, under the same guarantee?' 'Go ahead,' he said, so I told him joke number two. It concerns an Irish commercial traveller whose job involved long absences from home. He had an extremely pretty and rather flirtatious wife, a circumstance which caused him some anxious moments. One day, on his return home from a long trip, she opened the door and, radiant with happiness: said: 'Oh Patrick, I've got some wonderful news. We're going to have a baby.' At first Patrick felt he had won the Irish lottery but when the significance of her news dawned upon him, joy wrestled with suspicion. Finally, when suspicion overcame joy, he seized her by the shoulders and said angrily: 'Are you sure it's *yours*?' I bought the next round and was lucky to leave that Irish public house alive!

Incidentally, I found Mel Tormé of *Mountain Greenery* fame to be the most cultured popular entertainer I have ever met. A fine musical director, he knew exactly what he wanted from an orchestra and got it. I travelled the length of Ireland with this man, who seemed more like a university don than a pop star. His engagements took us to several sad little Irish towns on the way from Dublin to Belfast. In some of them acts of unspeakable wickedness had occurred. Yet it was a peaceful and lovely countryside we passed through, even though to me a certain awful melancholy hung like a cloud over the landscape.

Paddy the chauffeur, by the way, was my superior in his knowledge of opera and the great tenors. He knew recordings by such forgotten but superb artists as Gigli, Richard Tauber, Richard Crooks, Charles Kullman, F. Tagliavini, Jussi Björling, the great Germans Rudolf Schock and F. Wunderlich, Herbert Ernst Groh, Peter Anders, E. Caruso, the father of Italian tenors, di Stefano (glorious partner of Maria Callas) the Lieder specialist Karl Erb, and others lost from the current lists because of the 'over-hyping' of lesser talents who sell more. There is no golden age of tenors today. I do not have their recordings in my collection. Some record company should offer chauffeur Paddy a job! Only in a city like Moscow will you find chauffers as musically erudite as Paddy. Those Russian drivers know their Borodin and Rimsky Korsakof. They learned it all at the marvellous Bolshoi theatre.

CHAPTER 77

The Ship's Steward

I shall not forget my German shipmates on a voyage I made to South America and the Caribbean in 1980. Each morning around 10am they would unveil their dreadful *Würst* (dried sausage) and pour out their schnapps. Always they offered me both items, but I could not face the ship's motion and the würst, though I shared their schnapps. Our French steward, a quiet and rather sad man from Le Havre, paled visibly as he watched our Teutons tucking into a huge plate of assorted seafood, swilled down (literally) with great draughts of wine, sometimes red and white in succession! Our steward had a delightful sense of humour; he liked to wear funny hats and do little dances after meals. One day we were shocked to learn that he had tried to jump overboard. He had recently been widowed and was very worried indeed about his children. What a humane and kind man was Captain Bayonette! He visited our steward in the sickbay almost every hour until the end of the voyage, and one read in his face his concern for his crew member.

CHAPTER 78

'Oh Yes We Have No Bananas!'

The port of Limon in Costa Rica is the departure port for millions of bananas exported to Europe in the legendary banana boats. Modern ships, like the French freighter *Sans Souci*, have excellent refrigeration systems, ensuring the fruit arrives at its European port as fresh as when it left Costa Rica, one of the world's main suppliers.

It was fascinating to watch the bananas moving up in small crates on a moving band. For many hours an endless procession of bananas jostled one another in their crates, displaying an almost human impatience to get aboard and be stowed away. I watched bemused as this endless stream moved to its eventual conclusion. Soon, because time is money for these ships, the good ship *Sans Souci* would thrust her bows into the Atlantic and her cargo would be discharged in Hamburg or Le Havre, thence to be distributed to supermarkets in the major cities of Europe.

Aboard the French freighter, Sans Souci, *1982. Willie, ex-Paratrooper on right, the author, centre, share a drink with a French officer.*

CHAPTER 79

A Piscatorial Disaster,
or Better Luck Next Time

One afternoon I was leaning over the guardrail in Limon's harbour. My German shipmate had decided to do some fishing. Like most Germans, he was thorough and painstaking in all he undertook, so he used a state-of-the-art fishing rod and accessories. His tackle must have cost a small fortune, so elaborate and beautifully made was it. He fixed his bait, cast his line and, fully expectant, puffed a good cigar as he awaited results. I thought he might catch a whale with all that gear but . . . *nothing*!

A few feet away a West Indian docker, equipped with just a line, hook and bait, left the ship after about half an hour with a basketful of writhing, gleaming silver fish.

The German fisherman took his failure with a dignified shake of the head as he stowed away his tackle. '*Dass verstehe ich nicht!*' (I don't understand it), he kept muttering.

CHAPTER 80

Storm at Sea

In 1982 I was in a force 10 gale in the French ten thousand-ton freighter *Sans Souci* and as I watched in near terror the grey fusion, menacing and angry, of sea and sky, I felt frightened and uncomfortably close to my Maker. We all did. Waves as high as suburban houses rushed at the ship in seemingly endless succession and fury. The wind shrieked through the aerials and halyards and that wallowing, rolling, pitching ten thousand-tonner first stood on her stern, then toppled helplessly into a vast valley of water, only to rise and shudder yet again on the crest of another huge wave. I thought at one point that she would not come out of the depths again, that an avalanche of water would pour down her funnel, and that we would turn over and perish!

The French Captain, an elegant cultured gentleman, was a fine seaman who exuded calm and confidence at all times. Known, as is customary in the French Merchant Navy, as the Commandant, he declared quietly: 'I don't like this.' (the storm) 'We will skirt it and spend an extra day at sea.' When one considers the fact that for freighters cargo, time and money are the main factors to be taken into account, you can get some idea of the severity of that storm. Still . . . I would not have missed it for the world and I felt a kind of (immodest) pride in the fact that I stayed on my feet on this Gallic bucking bronco the whole time and did not miss a meal.

My two fellow passengers, both ex-German Army soldiers in World War II, and once members of Von Paulus's Army, were not to be seen for two days! I tried to console them by visits to their cabin, but all they wanted was to see, once more, the port of Hamburg. Both were what Americans call 'tough cookies'. One harangued me in mid-Atlantic, declaring that England was the cause of Europe's danger from the USSR. If we had made peace with Germany, all, so he believed, would have been well and the Red Menace would have been terminated once and for all. I reminded him that three times this century his fatherland had burst through its frontiers to murder and pillage; that in 1939 the Pope, the American President and the British Prime Minister had pleaded with Herr Hitler to vacate Poland, and suggested to him that the first bombs on Warsaw were the inevitable forerunners of those that destroyed the so-beautiful city of Dresden and other German cities. At one point I felt he might toss me over the side, yet in the end, we became good friends and I had a strange feeling he would have jumped overboard to save me!

CHAPTER 81

Russia

Some colleagues in London were scornful about doing business with the Russians. 'You will never get the money,' said some. 'You are wasting your time,' said others. They were all wrong!

The top management in the UK and in America showed prescience in realising that, although immediate benefits were not likely to be impressive, the long-term possibilities were enormous. They saw a vast new market of many, many millions, certain, one day, to open up to Western products. In exchange for Dame Shirley Bassey and Mr Paul Anka, we were able to offer the classical public in the UK marvellous performances by S. Richter of Chopin and other fine classical artists, both known and unknown. True, HMV (EMI) had relations with the state record firm *Melodya*, dating back to the beginning of recorded music. However, it was *United Artists Records* which saw and achieved close cooperation in the middle and popular repertoires, areas, rather neglected by EMI for many, many years. Unfortunately, the takeover of UA by EMI in 1980 put an end to the UA Eastern Bloc venture. It was a loss of mutual concern to UA and the Eastern record firms, nearly all of which did some business with UA.

The Russians honoured their contractual obligations to the letter. I found them professional and correct, but (initially) rather cold and hypersensitive. They dislike Western executives who 'ride a high horse' and are patronising. The Russians are a very tough and very proud people. History has inflicted awful suffering on them and, it seems, that is not over yet . . . McDonalds in Moscow (I'm joking, of course!).

It is a race against time. The reforms of Mr Yeltsin and Mr Putin must improve the living standards of the people soon or the 'bad guys', the old guard and associated extremists, will take over and it will be back to square one and a new and ominous era in Russian relations with the West.

It was a sweet moment when I waved a Russian cheque for US dollars in front of our Company's leading anti-Russian sceptic. He was a lovely chap but said, 'Get out of my office!' High comedy blends with despair in the Russian psyche.

After my Russian adventure, I think my happiest moment came when,

on retirement, I received a personal telegram from a high official in the
Russian music world wishing me a 'Long and happy retirement'. I drank
another vodka to that!

CHAPTER 82

Moscow

I am there for UA Records Ltd. Clutching a piece of paper with the
address of the State Publishing House on it, I step out of the car and
have some difficulty locating the correct building, where I have an
appointment. I see a gentleman in a black leather jacket and resolve to seek
his help. Suddenly a small and vicious mongrel dog is snarling and snapping
at my legs, barking loudly in protest at my presence. I stand absolutely still,
but the beastly animal sinks his molars into my (mercifully thick) trousers.
He bites through the serge but makes only minor indentations into my
lower leg. At last the owner (KGB?) calls him off and goes away. In the
hotel I see the doctor but he says, as the skin is not broken; all I need is a
dab of iodine. (Who told them I was a Lady Thatcher supporter?)

On first arriving in Moscow, I get a fright. I am with an official party of
British business people in the Soviet capital under the auspices of the
Anglo-Soviet Trade Mission. At the airport we file through Customs and
report to a young lady awaiting us at a desk to check off our names. On to
the hotel coach they all climb except me! I am taken to a small room, bare
except for a couple of chairs and a wooden table, and told to wait. Through
the window I see my companions (I heard later they were concerned about
me!) move off to the city.

An hour later the girl returns and hands me back my passport. 'You may
go to the hotel,' she says kindly and leads me to an *Intourist* car. 'What was
wrong?' I ask somewhat nervously. The young lady explains that my name
has been accidentally left off the list submitted by the Soviet Consulate in
London. All's well that ends well.

The journey from airport to city centre cannot be made without your
Russian *Intourist* guide pointing out the giant tank trap some ten or twelve
miles from the Kremlin. A mass of flowers under glass celebrates the place
where the German Army was stopped.

Now we are almost in sight of the Kremlin. It is a moving experience to
observe this spot and to remember how many brave Russians died here. As
for German casualties, it is hard to find sympathy for them. Twenty million
Russians died in World War II.

CHAPTER 83

Moscow in the Late 'Seventies

Hotel Ukraine

The Hotel Ukraine is vast. The restaurant area is reminiscent of Paddington Station – forlorn. The waiters, lacking the incentives available to their Western brothers, are in no great hurry to succour a weary traveller. They stand chanting to each other, seemingly indifferent to the needs of their guests. I used sometimes to wait twenty minutes or so trying to catch a merciful waiter's eye, but to no avail.

Desperate situations require radical solutions, so on one occasion I rose from my seat and went and KNELT, arms raised as though in prayer. It worked!

I was advised never to 'tip' a Russian in front of another Russian. However, I did discover one sure way to obtain fast service from waiters and chauffeurs. It was to leave, in an exposed place, a packet of Marlborough cigarettes.

A particularly agreeable driver was required to convey me to the offices of the State Record Company, *Melodya*. When I arrived there, I wrote down the time I estimated when I would need to be taken back to the hotel and the driver nodded to show he understood. However, my conversations with *Melodya* lasted much longer than intended and when I came out, my driver had departed, leaving me lost in a distant part of this great city and far from my hotel. I looked for one of the famous underground stations and for a bus stop – all to no avail. Then I saw a policeman and approached him. I showed my passport and told him my hotel. An extremely courteous young man, he said, 'Wait,' and disappeared. About five minutes later he returned with a taxi, opened the door for me and actually saluted! Such courtesy, such human warmth! At that moment I loved Moscow.

In the old Soviet Union sin was not allowed. That is why on every hotel floor a stern matron was posted, from whom one had to collect one's room key and to whom one had to hand it over on leaving.

These redoubtable ladies ensured that no one could transgress the sacred limits by admitting unauthorised visitors to his room. They kept an eagle eye on the guests and thus was Soviet public morality assured. In a comical way it recalled to my mind that notice on the wall of the rooms in 'Aggie Weston's' in Plymouth: 'Under no circumstances must more than one rating occupy this room!'

Perhaps I am the only member of the British record industry to have received a personal Christmas card from a member of the Supreme Soviet. It bears the signature of Mme. Irina Archipova, adored diva of the world-renowned Bolshoi Theatre Company.

Mme. Archipova gave a recital of songs by Pushkin at the Wigmore Hall, London and United Artists marked the occasion by releasing her album of songs by Russia's immortal poet, Pushkin.

I cannot read Russian, but in a strange way that seems not to matter too much when you hear that lovely velvet voice caressing the – to our ears – difficult vowels and consonants, whose hidden meanings are revealed to non-Russians as well as to her fellow countrymen. That fusion of romance and deep sadness gives those Pushkin songs a magical power over our emotions, a power which we do not quite understand and one that renders a literal comprehension of the texts unnecessary. As Mme. Archipova takes us on a musical journey to old Russia, we inevitably succumb. It is a Russia that, despite the horrors of the 20th Century, survives in modern Russia today.

A kind and gracious lady, an artiste one can never forget.

CHAPTER 84

Moscow Again, 1978-9

The Kremlin is so impressive a building that our eyes are reluctant to leave it. Every hour the plaintive tones of the Kremlin bell ring out and a corporal and two soldiers make a ceremonial march to Lenin's tomb. The Guards know precisely the number of steps required to reach the tomb, where the guard is changed in two swift movements. Like our Guards in London, these young Russian soldiers may remain still and statuesque for as long as one hour. I saw not a flicker on their faces nor a movement during the time I stood close to the tomb of Lenin.

It was touching to see young married couples, fresh from their nuptials, walking hand in hand to place bouquets of flowers.

At the other end of Red Square stands the great church of St Basil. No longer used as a church, its unusual architecture holds the viewer enthralled. At sunset it is a breathtaking experience to watch the sun sink behind those cupolas or onion-like roofs, clustered and tinged with a gorgeous blend of red, gold, yellow, purple and silver – truly a magnificent sight.

The overall impression of these historic buildings is of harmony, grace and magnificence. Once one has seen the Bell Tower of Ivan The Great, the Cathedral of the Annunciation and the Kremlin, one can never forget them.

In the Palace of Congresses, added to the Kremlin buildings in 1960/1961, there are more than 800 rooms and the splendid auditorium accommodates 600 people. It is the largest in the world. Many centuries and several cultures have flowed over the Kremlin walls, within which twenty tall towers stand witness to the fact that this was once a great fortress. Five of these towers are crowned with shining ruby stars. The impression is stunning and they are arresting symbols of this great city.

Another jewel of rare beauty inside the Kremlin is the lovely single-domed church of The Deposition of The Robe built at the same time as the Annunciation. It is small and has a graceful elegance all its own.

CHAPTER 85

Vive la France

Long ago I made a journey on the tube with my daughter Nicolette, now a married lady and mother of our two grandsons. I went with her to Victoria to meet a young French pen friend who was to stay with us for a holiday, in return for a holiday in France with Annick's family the previous year. My daughter, until recently a French and Latin teacher at the St Paul's Cathedral (London) Choir School, was a good French speaker even as a teenager, so they were soon gossiping at a furious rate to the accompaniment of much giggling. We travelled home to Ealing in a tube carriage full of business types, both male and female, the former engrossed in their newspapers and the latter in their fashion or romantic magazines. The silence was broken when Annick suddenly said in her heavily accented English: 'Vot is zis verd I have heard on ze boat . . . Fooking?'

Glasses fell off noses and our passengers were, to put it mildly, shocked. However, in several cases, embarrassment gave way to mirth and there were many chuckles. Certainly Annick banished boredom on that tube journey! Today there would be no red faces at the use of the once dreaded 'F' word. Even young children use it.

Our daughter Nicolette on left with a French friend, Annick.

CHAPTER 86

Stettin, Poland

During the inter-War years our ship visited Stettin, a city in which almost everyone except old ladies wore a uniform. We saw little girls and boys in Hitler uniforms, but were unaware of the evil that caused World War II.

We thought the children were the equivalent of our Scouts and Guides. We were amused by the frequent sight on the streets of people greeting each other with arm raised in the Hitler salute and on board many sailors thought it a bit of a lark to greet a shipmate in the same manner. This caused the following notice to appear on the ship's notice board:

> The practice of giving the Hitler salute must cease
> forthwith as it is likely to cause offence on shore.

Incidentally, we had our photos taken with a group of brown shirts who bought us several pints of excellent local beer in big German glasses.

We knew it not, but horror was waiting just a few months away.

CHAPTER 87

Hoots Mon!

In the 60's and 70's there was a daily TV show. I believe it was called *The One O'Clock Show* and it was televised from Glasgow's famous Theatre Royal. Record men regarded an appearance on it by one of their artists as a major 'plug' and the show was hosted by that very genial, but very professional, compère, Mr Larry Marshall. If your latest record featured on the show, chart success was a virtual certainty.

I made several trips to Glasgow to accompany artists due to appear. It enabled me to learn how our dear old Scots are libelled when described as 'mean'. Even though the company always gave me a generous entertainment allowance, I invariably returned to London with almost as much money as I had when I had set out for Glasgow. Those Scots would not allow you to put your hand in your pocket. I enjoyed my visits and Scottish hospitality enormously – and so did the artists.

Thus I am qualified to refute those false charges of parsimony. I told a number of jokes in a Glasgow bar and was rewarded with 'Have another drink, laddie' and hoots of laughter. I hope, dear reader, you too will smile if I place a few of them on record.

Why do Scots bagpipers walk up and down when playing the pipes? . . . Because a moving target is harder to hit!

A Scotsman went into Selfridges in Oxford Street and asked for the haberdashery counter. On arrival there, he asked the young lady assistant for twenty thimbles. 'Good gracious, Sir,' said the young lady, 'You must be doing a lot of sewing.' 'Och, nee, lassie,' answered the Scotsman, 'We're just having a wee party!'

Nor is it true that if you forget your change leaving a Scottish shop, the shopkeeper will tap on the window with a sponge!

A Scotsman took his little son to church for the first time. As they walked home after the service, the father said, 'How did you like the service, son?' The wee laddie replied, 'Och, it was very guid, Daddy. I got half a croon – how much did you get?'

According to tradition, it is lucky if, when crossing the Forth Bridge, you throw a coin into the water beneath. Scotsmen, it's said, always have the coin on a piece of string! If that is so, I expect they do the same when tossing a coin into the Trevi Fountain in Rome. Dear readers, I can vouch for the fact that this is another example of Sassanach perfidy.

I have another memory of the Forth Bridge. HMS *Leander* was passing under the famous bridge and I happened to be aloft tying in the Admiral's flag. I saw, just a few feet above my head, several of the rivets that hold that splendid bridge together. I could almost touch the bridge as we slid smoothly up river.

'We'll tak' a cup o' kindness yet, for auld lang syne' Do not let those devious politicians separate us, Jock!

CHAPTER 88

Singapore

Of all our former colonies, I believe that Singapore is the one of which we can be most proud.

Since achieving independence as a city state, the Singaporeans have created a society that is a model for the world. Multi-racial, though predominantly Chinese, it maintains complete racial harmony and we British should envy the inhabitants of Singapore their judiciary. In this place the punishment fits the crime. The law is applied to all and thus there is little serious crime in Singapore. Villains do not leave court with a smile, as they so often do in politically-correct Britain. Magistrates and judges administer the law properly and the people are thus protected. One recent example amply illustrates this.

A certain young American thought he would amuse himself by vandalising cars. He was sentenced to six strokes of the cane, and not withstanding a Presidential appeal for clemency, his American posterior was duly whacked. I doubt whether that young man is much interested in vandalism these days

In the 'thirties rickshaws abounded and at noon one saw their owners, those very slim but agile young men, crouched beside their rickshaws eating a bowl of rice. Their stamina was amazing as they conveyed mostly Europeans and service personnel about the city. In 1982, when I returned, I saw no rickshaws, only smart taxis.

These clever and industrious people have built a fine international airport on land they have reclaimed from the sea. As they have little space to expand outwards, they build fine high-rise flats and office blocks.

Another remarkable achievement is the transformation of the former Royal Naval Dockyard into one of the world's most important ship repair yards. Singapore, with its fine harbour, is a kind of maritime Clapham Junction of the East. You will see flags of every major nation flying from the sterns of ships in a harbour always crowded with vessels.

The famous Raffles Hotel remains firm in my memory, for though as an ordinary sailor I could not afford those world-famous cocktails served in the bar, I did once witness an unforgettable sight. As I stood outside the Raffles, who should emerge through the main entrance but Charles

Chaplin and a gloriously beautiful Miss Paulette Goddard. Mr Chaplin and his lady got into a rickshaw and set off on a tour of the city. Miss Goddard wore a stunning white dress with a large white wide-brimmed hat. Mr Chaplin was immaculate in a white tropical suit.

We Naval signalmen and telegraphists were – dare I say it – the intelligentsia of the lower deck. We could actually do joined-up writing and spell. In off-duty times we wore white suits bought from Chinese tailors for five Singapore dollars (5 x 2 shillings and four pence in those days). We called ourselves the five-dollar gentlemen and used to frequent the *Old World* and *New World* dance halls, where for a dollar a ticket you could ask delightful young Chinese girls to dance. They were very tempting in their long dresses with slits down the sides, and when they walked you could glimpse a lovely slim white leg. Oh what a beautiful life it was – soon to end in tragedy when the Japanese invaded!

Gentlemen, be careful if you take wives or sweethearts to Singapore! The shops are magnificent and stocked full with all kinds of wares from Europe, Japan and the United States.

I am happy to tell you that cricket is still played on the green outside St Andrew's Cathedral, the Anglican main presence and strongly reminiscent of a large parish church in some small English town. When Sir G. Raffles went to Singapore. it was a swamp. I found the people I met in 1982 very warm and not unwilling to acknowledge their heritage from this small island – for me the centre of the universe, England.

In the 1930's the Royal Navy had a signal station on the roof of the Hong Kong Shanghai Bank building on the waterfront of Singapore Harbour. I was a member of the signal staff. The SNO (Senior Naval Officer), Singapore had an office there.

After my watch, I headed for the lift and was just in time to enter before the door closed. To my surprise and dismay, I found the only other occupant of the lift was the Commodore himself, the most senior Naval officer in the colony. On my best behaviour, I saluted and pressed the button for the ground floor. A slight downward movement suddenly halted and we were marooned between floors.

The Commodore betrayed no major signs of annoyance, but I felt rather nervous. How long would we have to stay imprisoned in this small box; it was hot and sticky. A hearty voice, obviously unaware of the VIP passenger shouted, 'Don't worry, Bunts (Signalman), we'll soon have you out of there.' I thought it wise to let our Royal Marine guard know who was in the lift, so I called 'The Commodore is in the lift. Please hurry.' Silence! Moments later our Marine, using a voice a bit like that of the chaplain, said, 'Kindly press the button'. We did and were on the way to the ground . . . As the door opened and the Commodore stepped out, he said kindly, 'Are you all right?' 'Yes, Sir,' I replied and with a nod he left for his car.

CHAPTER 89

Lifts

After a visit to HMS *Belfast*, secured over the River Thames at the Tower of London, my brother Billy, my son Philip, a young man and his girlfriend and I entered a lift in a nearby multi-storey car park.

It was a small lift and we were rather too close to each other – uncomfortably so. The door closed and my son pressed the button so that we could find our car on the fifth floor. The lift shuddered, moved a few feet and STOPPED!

It would not budge. We jumped up and down and kept pressing the knobs – to no avail. It was about 5 o'clock in the evening and we could see the lower legs of people hurrying home for the weekend break. We were sweating a little and frightened too, for no one seemed to notice when we pressed the alarm and we felt helpless and abandoned. The young lady was showing early signs of mounting hysteria; her head was moving from side to side and she could not keep still. Her boyfriend calmed her but panic was beginning to affect us all. Fear and despair grew by the minute . . . Outside it became ominously quiet and there was scarcely any movement.

The prospect of being left in that lift over night or longer made our nervous tension rise fast and if someone (may God bless them) had not heard our cries, I think it would have ended in tragedy. After about twenty minutes firemen arrived, and when we saw their big boots and helmets, relief overwhelmed us. I think claustrophobia is one of the most dreadful of human afflictions.

One good thing came out of this ordeal. I realised I had a very brave, very kind son. His calmness even in our most frightening moments gained the gratitude of all. To this day I fear lifts and always walk up and down by the stairs so as to avoid them.

CHAPTER 90

Turkish Delight

We are in an airport lounge awaiting our flight to Frankfurt-on-Main. An official announcement informs us that we shall be delayed because of a technical fault on the aircraft.

Resigned to a long wait, we are eventually taken to board a Turkish jet and on board we find several Turkish passengers, including some veiled ladies already seated, and some turbanned gentlemen looking very fierce and dignified.

I find myself seated next to a dear little old lady who is very frightened. Her son next to her holds her hand and it is quite touching to notice how he comforts her, reassuring her that she is safe.

I feel as if I were heading for Ankara, for the spirit of that ancient people pervades the aircraft. Then something extraordinary happens. They switch on the aircraft's audio system and, bursting upon my astonished ears, comes the sound of an old British Music Hall favourite, 'On Mother Kelly's Doorstep'!

To hear this hoary old favourite in such a place, at such a time and in such company seems to me the very height of absurdity and for a few moments I shake with inner laughter. My companions must think: 'that Englishman is MAD!'

It's a strange world! Someone aboard that plane has helped himself to my Burberry raincoat. I only hope it is keeping someone dry on the streets of Ankara or Istanbul.

CHAPTER 91

Barcelona, 1978

The cathedral in Barcelona is majestic and strikingly beautiful. On the steps one serenely lovely evening I watched an unforgettable example of the Seguilla dance.

Several family groups, ranging from tiny children to adults old and young, formed circles and, to the soft tones of a small band of street musicians, they began to sway slightly, moving in a circle holding hands. At first they were dancing to a slow tempo; gradually it increased, raising the excitement of the dance. Faster and faster they went until the whole family circle was revelling in the fury of the dance.

As the sun went down behind that noble and imposing cathedral, one drank in the very spirit of old Catalonia, a culture as rich and fervent as the wine they drink and the songs and dances which are the very essence of all their lives.

CHAPTER 92

Poland, Sopot

Each year an international music festival is held in the Polish resort of Sopot; artists and musicians as well as music-business executives from Eastern and Western Europe attend, as well as participants from many countries of the world.

Under a Polish referee, votes are cast for the best performances and best songs in various categories. For example, 'Best Female Vocalist', 'Best Male Vocalist', 'Best New Group'. It is a truly international occasion.

I was a member of the international jury and found myself elected as a member of the committee responsible for counting the votes. As the counting proceeded, I noticed that frequently the Soviet artists seemed to be beating the USA and Britain into second or third place and I casually commented to the Polish referee, 'The Russians seem to be doing well.' With a smile he said, 'Yes, like the rest of us, they like to win'.

Present at Sopot was the very popular Head of Radio Luxembourg, Geoffrey Everett. We played a trick on him, but before I tell that tale let me remind readers that this was a time when the Cold War was at its height and suspicion was rife, both of the West on the part of the Russians and of the Russians on the part of the Western countries. We saw a KGB man under every hotel bed and in every bar and restaurant. I hope that explanation will enable you to enjoy the joke played on the hapless Geoffrey Everett.

A Pole who was a fluent Russian speaker conspired with us in compiling a letter in Russian and placed it in Geoffrey's pigeonhole at the hotel reception.

The letter said:

We are watching you. Please obey following instructions – it would not be wise to ignore our wishes.

In each voting category you must vote as under:

1. USSR	1. USSR	1. USSR
2. GDR	2. Latvia	2. Korea
3. USA	3. Gt Britain	3. Japan

You may vary this order slightly and on occasion include a country such as

Spain or Switzerland, but such countries must never rise above 3rd, 4th or 5th position.

The USA cannot rise above 2nd place.

We shall watch you closely and will monitor your votes.'

Geoffrey found our Russian-speaking Pole and this merry fellow sat down with a drink and, with feigned gravity, translated the 'KGB' message. The chief executive of Radio Luxembourg was no fool and soon realised he was on the wrong end of a joke. It would need more than the KGB to upset imperturbable Geoffrey Everett.

I wonder whether Geoffrey ever discovered the identity of the initiator of this 'spoof'? Perhaps, you, dear reader, can name him!!

Later that day I had a nocturnal swim in a Baltic sea lit up by moonlight, which covered the waters in a veil of silver. My German colleague and I were amazed how warm it was as we floated around in Neptune's domain.

CHAPTER 93

Warsaw, 1977

The Polish capital is now a small but charming city, rebuilt brick by brick by those indestructible Poles after the almost total destruction of the city by the Germans, who bombarded Warsaw with artillery and merciless air attacks. Thousands were killed and survivors were driven into the sewers.

Today the town square is a peaceful place, which has fully regained its former old-world charm. I was moved by the spectacle of a people who, despite unimaginable woes, could still fill their churches to overflowing for Sunday Mass. I saw them kneeling in the street because there was insufficient room for them inside the church.

A 'must' for every Warsaw visitor is a call at that lovely church wherein it is said the heart of Chopin, that prince of the pianoforte, rests. Another delight the visitor may experience is a walk along the banks of the Vistula. Then he may end his day with vodka or an excellent coffee sitting quietly outside a café in that beautiful town square.

We British have many thousands of Poles in our midst. We should consider ourselves fortunate for, whilst retaining their religion and culture, they integrate perfectly with the indigenous population of our island. They keep our laws and are more patriotic than many of their fellow citizens.

Perhaps the city which best personifies the soul of the Polish nation is lovely old Krakow, once the seat of kings. A proud but deeply melancholy atmosphere broods over the ancient palace. This is a city which, once visited, is quite unforgettable. The visitor is transported back centuries as he walks its historic streets. It avoids a great part of the vulgarity that afflicts most western cities. May they, the Poles, live at last in peace.

CHAPTER 94

Paris, tu n'as pas Changé

Paris Mid '70's

On a visit to our Paris office I was introduced to the vivacious daughter of that fine Armenian-French artist, Charles Aznavour. This young lady took me on a tour in her small motorcar of that lovely and romantic city.

It proved to be a hair-raising experience, in the course of which, several times, I thought I would end up in the mortuary! French drivers are notorious for their almost permanent state of road rage but this young lady drove as though the *rues* of Paris were her exclusive domain; there were many angry exchanges as we swirled around the Place de la Concorde in a veritable sea of automobiles. Fist-shaking and some rather rude gestures were exchanged as we fought for survival. No French driver seemed willing to give way, and so we had some furious encounters. All this Madamoiselle Aznavour suffered with truly Gallic *sang froid*; I got out of her car a nervous wreck but with a happy memory of a very charming and amusing young lady.

I heard later that she fell in love with an American musician and went to live in Los Angeles.

Of her Father's many 'hits', my favourite will always be 'She'.

On another occasion in the French capital I was taken to lunch in a restaurant just off the Champs Elysées. It specialised in beef steaks, but I felt distinctly ill at ease to see, on each wall, large pictures of bovine heads, so arranged that you could not avoid their reproachful gaze as you devoured your delicious steak.

The waiters seemed to feel malicious enjoyment when they realised our discomfort. Those Frenchmen have a weird sense of humour!

Now I know how it feels to be a cannibal – *guilty*!

CHAPTER 95

Yugoslavia in the 'Seventies

I made several visits to Yugoslavia and my journeys took me to the Capital, Belgrade, to Zagreb, Sarejevo and the quaint cobbled streets of Dubrovnik. The town used to be a bastion against the raiders from the east and had a narrow beach along the Adriatic.

It was moving to stand approximately on the spot in Sarajevo where the assassination of the Archduke became the catalyst for the slaughter of World War I.

My friend Dusan took me to the Moslem area, and we walked down a narrow street where little men in fezzes were busy with small hammers making coffee sets for tourists. I saw absolutely no signs of racial tension. Everything seemed normal, and back in busy Belgrade all appeared just as it was in any other European capital. Little did Dusan and I know of the awful days ahead for Serbs, Croats and Moslems.

I was privileged to be in Yugoslavia with that grand old man of jazz, Mr Dizzy Gillespie. The founder of Be-bop and honoured veteran of American jazz, Mr Gillespie was the ideal artiste to tour with, always on time for airport departures and scrupulously professional on every occasion. He was greatly appreciated by audiences and by all with whom he came into contact.

Disaster overtook me on that tour. I should explain that the forward dates of our itinerary were financed by the revenues from the concerts. Hotel bills and air tickets were, as a rule on this tour, paid from concert takings. Our problem arose from the fact that the Yugoslav dinar was not accepted, so that to pay our way, we needed US dollars, British pounds or deutschmarks.

It was illegal to take Yugoslav currency out of the country, and as you passed through airport controls, you were asked whether you were aware of that law. In my case I answered in the affirmative and shivering inwardly, I passed into the departure lounge, feeling I had got away with it. I was stopped just as I was about to board and there, in my suitcase, was a wad of dinars. I, together with the promoter, had hoped that we could get enough dinars out to change in London for an acceptable currency to pay the costs of our forward dates.

As I was arrested, I was just able to call out my home telephone number to that kind lady of Jazz, Annie Ross. 'Tell my wife I'm delayed, please', I shouted. As soon as she landed at Heathrow, Miss Ross informed my wife.

On arriving at Police Headquarters in Belgrade, I was put in a room to await questioning and in the care of a young Serb policeman with whom I played noughts and crosses and cards. He had little English and I no Serbian, so conversation was limited. He was, to my surprise, very affable and the fact that I could have been a real villain seemed to make no difference to him.

I was held for two days and was treated very well by the Serb police. Comical as it may sound, I was getting rather attached to them, especially my young guard. I was given my passport back and told to leave the country. I could have been held for a very long time and was extremely fortunate. If I had gone to prison, people would have said "Serb' you right!!'

In Belgrade I sat on a seat close to a very pretty girl. I saved that young lady from being attacked by a man – *I controlled myself!*

CHAPTER 96

Ravenna in Italy, 1978

I was sipping my cappuccino in a café in Ravenna as Mozart's *Eine kleine Nachtmusik* drifted across the town square on a light summer breeze. Ravenna, that venerable and most ancient city, shrieks of the long-vanished centuries, for this place was a major Christian citadel even before the fifth century. It gave the Church two saints: St Appolinaris, martyr and Bishop of Ravenna, and one of Christendom's most illustrious Fathers, St Peter Chrysologos, Archbishop of that city in the mid-fifth century.

This great early theologian was, in his youth, deacon to Bishop Cornelius of adjacent Imola. His teacher and mentor, Cornelius, took St Peter to Rome, where Pope Sixtus, brushing aside other eminent candidates for the Ravenna Archbishopric, appointed St Peter Chrysologos.

It is not possible to exaggerate the importance of this St Peter, for his doctrinal writings, some still extant, are one of the supreme pillars of Catholic orthodoxy. Together with his contemporaries, St Augustine and St Jerome, he caused Christianity to take a giant step forward and their voices reach down the centuries to us today. By virtue of their antiquity, the witness and testimonies of these early Fathers assumed a special validity for, and relevance to, us in this frenetic modern world.

St Peter Chrysologos drew ecstatic congregations in an age of profound faith. They believed that God himself was addressing them through the golden eloquence of their Archbishop. In a strange way I saw in my imagination the jubilant crowd listening to his perorations in this very square.

Ah! On a dais across the square do I not see the Emperor Valentinian III, the Empress Placidia and their children listening intently to their Archbishop, whose episcopal consecration was greeted by the people of Ravenna with jubilation and thanksgiving? The images in my mind fade and Mozart too is silent. I walk slowly across the square, where, in an alley just off the square, I find *a sex shop*!

Note: For the historical information given here I am indebted to *Butler's Lives of the Saints.*

CHAPTER 97

Bulgaria

I have something dreadful to tell you about the good citizens of Sofia. *They do not drink tea!*

One sunny Sunday afternoon I took a stroll though the centre of this pleasant city. I admired the charming little Russian church and, as a former choirboy, I was curious to peep inside and puzzled when I could find no choir stalls, for the interior was circular and, to Western eyes, rather quaint. A lady was cleaning the floor and looked at me with, I thought, a rather disapproving eye, so I left and entered a pretty little park alive with multi-coloured blooms. There I took a seat and watched children at play, with their parents basking in the sun.

Suddenly I was overwhelmed with an insistent desire for a cup of tea. Oh how I yearned for that heavenly British 'cuppa'! I decided to see whether I could find a café or restaurant that could provide so great a comfort for a fellow so far from home.

I tried several places without success, but in a hotel a friendly young waiter said, 'I bring you tea'. Overjoyed, I waited for his return.

At last he appeared with a tray. It contained no friendly teapot, but just a cup containing a greenish-looking fluid with tiny green leaves floating in it. Gingerly I took a sip. Good heavens, what a taste, and what an aroma of exotic flowers! I did not want to appear ungrateful to a waiter who sincerely wanted to help, so I carried on sipping until he was out of sight, after which I paid the bill. Undrinkable! I did not get a decent cup that day.

Since then a Bulgarian friend has taken me to task. It seems that it is no longer true that one cannot obtain a cup of tea. I hope I may be forgiven!

Sofia is a small capital, but green and beautiful. Some new buildings lack distinction from an architectural point of view, but the overall impression of Sofia is of an extremely modern city, yet one which still retains its romantic antiquity.

The Bulgarians now live under a relaxed régime and it is a happy country, adjusting itself to the rapid technological changes, yet without sacrificing those human values that are essential to a decent civilised society. In this it differs from some countries I could mention.

Bulgaria's natural resources are those of a small country, but she is rich indeed in cereals, fruit, vines, sunflowers, strawberries, and it has some tobacco.

It is, however, the tourist facilities, equal to any in Europe, that are Bulgaria's greatest source of revenue. The Black Sea coast runs in a glorious curve from Antopol through mile upon mile of superb beaches to Varna and beyond. Golden beaches, where the visitor can seek out his own personal spot and where his children may disport themselves in safety. All the way from Bourgas to the River Danube, the amenities are superb.

People in the West are gradually beginning to recognise that this small country is a veritable paradise, where a warm welcome awaits individuals or families. For the perfect holiday it is the perfect choice.

Off the beaten tourist track is the breathtakingly lovely Valley of Roses in the Kazanluk region and the mountain range known as the Balkans.

I have to say that the Black Sea is not black . . . it is a heavenly blue!

CHAPTER 98

Dachau

I visited Dachau in 1976. We were in Munich for concerts with an American band, and someone told the young men from Los Angeles that they were near the notorious concentration camp Dachau. At once they expressed a keen interest to visit it. So we left the Munich Hilton and made the short car journey to that place of death. As we stepped through the entrance, we became aware of a feeling of immense sadness and melancholy. A guide escorted us through the low building where, under the pretext of being sent to take a shower, the men, women and children were slowly gassed.

An atmosphere of recent horror hung over the place like a pall and one felt a shiver of anguish that such wickedness could exist among our human kind. What sort of beings could do such acts?

A Synagogue and a Catholic Chapel have now been built inside Dachau. To pray in such a place would, for me at least, be to shake a fist of indignation at the Almighty.

It was a very subdued party of young Americans who returned to the Munich Hilton.

On that day we all heard, in the remote recesses of our beings, the screams and cries of Dachau's victims . . . and the stench of Evil gnawed at our guts.

PART VII

Political and Social Comment

CHAPTER 99

The Virus of Political Correctness

Ordinary men and women are largely oblivious to the virus of Political Correctness. They are, of course, familiar with the ugly and anti-social terms, 'having sex', 'gay' and 'partner'. The PC virus is gnawing away at the very vitals of Western civilization. The implications for the future are very sinister indeed. As Cilla Black says in her show, *Blind Date*, 'Let's find out, shall we?'

Sufferers from the virus have their brains so addled that they are no longer able to make objective judgements in accordance with the natural order. This is having dire consequences. Consider, please, the following:

Some gifted medical scientists are pursuing lines of research that are utterly depraved. They bring humanity down to a level beyond even that of Hitler or Stalin. They are cloning animals – tomorrow will it be humans? Even more dreadful, some of them condone – no, positively encourage – sad, infertile women to achieve pregnancy by indulging in methods of procreation that are deeply degrading. All they need, the clever fellows tell us, is a bucket, a syringe and a drop of any old partner's sperm. At this point we truly touch rock bottom. It is time the big bomb dropped. Yet there are women who, so that they may conceive as and when they wish, intend to have their eggs' frozen! Good God, where will it end, PC women?

PC victims cannot recognize the gender difference. To them a man is a woman and a woman is a man. They are interchangeable in all situations and professions. What a nonsense! Such people expectorate in the face of God.

Another nasty manifestation of the virus is the despicable compensation culture. Fall down in the street and it's not your fault for not looking where you are going. Rather it's the Council's. Sue it and enrich a greedy lawyer, and be awarded a ridiculous sum of money as compensation, money paid out of your fellow citizens' taxes. Is that not a sophisticated way of stealing a wallet? Huge sums are paid out annually by PC sick tribunals, sometimes on the orders of the European Union Court in Luxembourg, whose rule now brushes aside that of British Law. Are we insane? Is Britain becoming an asylum?

Social workers, many of them smitten with the virus of Political

Correctness, often have to take difficult decisions in cases where, whatever they decide, it will be denounced as unjust. In such cases we should be very restrained in our criticisms. However, many Labour Councils are so badly infected with the PC virus that they make decisions of breath-taking idiocy. They cannot wait for the removal of Clause 28 from the Statute Book. Clause 28 – intended to protect the innocence of young children from homosexual propaganda! Why? The question answers itself.

Another example of PC folly is the counselling culture. In my youth, when grief came, as come it must to all of us at some time, we wept in private and drew comfort from members of our families, from priests, or from close friends. Those in sorrow today often have no family, no priest and no friends. Instead they lay bare their most personal secrets to a stranger, a PC counsellor, often untrained.

PC teachers want to cut our children off from their country's history. PC examiners are said to intend to discriminate against public school students when marking, and the PC academics in Oxford are said to have the intention of likewise discriminating against the top schools, who have long been a main source of supply for the universities. If this PC stupidity is allowed to prevail, our once-famous universities will, within a decade, sink down to second-rate mediocrity. That awful virus again! Are we the only nation in the world in which education is a political football? No wonder our youngsters are far behind other nations in academic achievement, especially in languages. In Paris, Brussels, Moscow and several other cities, I have met young people with whom I found no difficulty in discussing world affairs, yet who maintained, at the same time, a lively interest in our pop music and artists. Most had at least two other languages besides their own. Our young people are as bright as any in the world, but because the educational Establishment is dominated by and obsessed with Political Correctness, they are being robbed of their birthright.

In this new educational Establishment of ours, the PC academics and New Labour Council Educational Authorities postulate the absurd doctrine that students who fail examinations are damaged and made to suffer unfair stress. Twaddle! Without failure, success has no point. If a student fails 'A' Levels, it is far from the end of the world. Let him remember the old proverb, 'Try, try and try again'. To make examinations easy for the sake of avoiding failures is downright silly. In that case, why bother to have examinations at all? We even hear talk of introducing a slightly easier degree course, presumably so that everyone can pass!

It is, however, in the area, so vitally important as it is, of moral and sexual relations, that the PC virus has inflicted the most massive damage on the quality of life of all of us. The protagonists of PC hate marriage and tell our young people that is is old-fashioned and irrelevant to modern people. To such PC pundits, who throng the media and particularly the pages of our popular press, terms such as 'love' and 'commitment for life' are anathema. Have you, dear reader, ever examined the magazines on offer in supermarkets and stores such as those of W.H. Smith? Have you been revolted and nauseated by the blatant sexual enticements offered to young girls, with headlines such as 'How to increase your orgasms', 'How to make your partner (never lover!) happy in bed'? These sex-obsessed publications are expertly produced and beautifully printed in fine colour – all designed to tempt, allure and arouse, and presumably to awaken sexual desire in impressionable young women. A plague on the houses of those who perpetrate and publish all such pernicious rubbish. They are mostly women editors, themselves seriously ill with the virus.

Why do they not teach their readers about real love? Of the gift of a committed lifelong man with whom to share their life? Why not teach them about real romance? About the importance of the family, about the depths of love and mutual support that are possible between a man and a woman – 'till death do us part'?

Walk down any high street, stroll through any supermarket, and you will see the consequences of the virus expressed in sartorial terms. Rarely indeed does one encounter a nicely dressed, truly feminine woman. Instead the modern women try to look like men, their upper bodies garbed in dreadful tops and their lower limbs in either jeans or – even worse! – trousers. Many of the older ladies look like laundry bags tied round the middle.

Is there a cure for the PC virus? YES THERE IS! As a first step, victims should read Kipling's poem, *If* every day. Before going to sleep, they should also read the following words – filled with such a depth of wisdom! – by Alexander Pope (1688-1744). Some may need longer than others to recover, but a cure is certain!

> First follow *Nature* and your judgement frame
> By her just standard, which is still the same,
> unerring *Nature*, still divinely bright,
> One clear, unchang'd and universal light,
> Life, force, and beauty, must to all impart,
> At once the source, and end, and test of Art.
>
> A. Pope

Dear PC readers, do not try to change the natural order, which comes from a source greater than ourselves.

CHAPTER 100

The BBC

Broadcasting House has as its adjacent buildings, Western House, home of Radio 2 and Egton House, home of Radio 1. As a former frequent visitor to any and all of these, I am, more than many, in a position to testify to the profound change of quality which the Corporation has undergone.

Broadcasting House itself dominates Upper Regent Street like the bows of a great ocean liner. In my day, as I entered, I felt as though I were walking into a great cathedral. Dignity and a reverential quiet pervaded the large reception area, while high above the main reception desk inspired Latin words were inscribed, proclaiming the BBC's mandate to spread Truth and Beauty to all peoples.

I speak of the period running roughly from the late 'forties up to the mid-'fifties, when the first portents of the terrible changes in the BBC appeared. They heralded the advent of the Rock revolution, headed by those talented Beatles, Elvis Presley, and The Rolling Stones. Before they appeared on the scene, the BBC was enjoying the final days in which its reputation for integrity and the highest possible standards in public broadcasting was global. Older readers will recall those stirring opening bars of Beethoven's Fifth Symphony, which preceded wartime news bulletins.

Sometimes the news was very bad indeed, but the BBC gave it without fudge, just factually as it was and totally true. In consequence the whole world, in those days, listened and believed.

Not so today! The BBC, especially in recent times, has sunk deep into a slough of squalid programmes and second-rate, often biased, political comment. It still does magnificent recreations of great classic novels, and still retains a few of its former successes. Nevertheless, it has suffered a drastic drop in its share of viewers and listeners. Mediocrity is the BBC today. That PC virus again! The great Sir John Reith is spinning in his grave.

CHAPTER 101

Join my *Fatwa* Against Political Correctness

1. Reject that awful word 'partner' and use instead whichever of the following terms is appropriate:
   Sweetheart, boyfriend, girlfriend, fiancé or fiancée or husband or wife!

2. Do not use the word 'gay' in its highjacked context.

3. Protest when PC-infected judges, magistrates and social workers pass sentences on villains which defy justice and common sense. No more Caribbean holidays for rascals who are anti-social. Almost daily one reads of sentences which allow the rogues to leave court with a smirk on their faces.

4. Have nothing to do with the wretched compensation culture, which enriches greedy lawyers at taxpayers' expense. There are very few occasions when a claim for compensation is justified. Only in the case of flagrant negligence should claims be made and then not in five or six figures. Remember that Wren who a year or so ago walked off with £30,000 for wrongful dismissal from the Royal Navy? She knew when she joined she would have to leave if she became pregnant. Our feeble government and the M.O.D. bowed before the EU Court and paid her!

5. Counselling is another PC racket. If sadness comes, bear it with dignity. If you have no family, no friends or priest to comfort, then weep alone. We all need a shoulder to cry on at some point, but you should not have to pay for it.

6. Do not permit, under any circumstances, the exposure of your children to so-called sex education by people who are not qualified to give it. If Mr Blair succeeds in his fanatical determination to abolish Clause 28, impose you own personal Clause 28. Tell social workers and teachers your child must not participate in such lessons. Let children keep their innocence. In cases where the home is bad and proper advice at the right age is unavailable, then a very careful choice must be made as to who should help the child concerned.

7. There are good and bad teachers. Ensure that your children are told

about our history. PC teachers hate our past, with the result that we have many children today who know about Nelson Mandela, but have never heard of Horatio, the Admiral who saved Britain from precisely the same danger of Euro-domination that faces us in the current scene. Children should be proud of Britain and especially of England, its beating heart.

Let the young have their 'pop' music, but teach also Mozart, Beethoven and the other masters. There is room in life for both.

Teach them too Shakespeare, Byron, Shelley, Keats, Pope as well as William Blake and Kipling. We are becoming a nation of yobs and morons. Look at some of today's pop icons, visitors to Mr Blair at No. 10 – and wring your hands in shame and fear.

8. A minor PC irritation is the expression 'met with'. If you meet someone, you must have been with them so why 'met with'?

9. Particularly revolting is the common usage of that ugly and demeaning phrase 'having sex', as though it were something one took off the supermarket shelf.

Say 'making love' instead. That has a more beautiful and civilised tone to it. Do people who 'have sex' love each other?

So dear reader resolve to combat PC wherever you find it. Ridicule and defy it. Or, shall we sink to the bottom of the barrel among the nations? The Monarchy, Parliament and The Church are all under attack.

CHAPTER 102

Mr Blair and the European Union

I believe our Prime Minister is a good and decent man who, with the best of intentions, is following a path which will reduce Britain (including Scotland and Wales) to the status of unimportant eastern provinces of that ghastly monster, a European Federation ruled by unelected European Commissioners in Brussels.

My Blair actually believes, in all sincerity, that our future lies in Europe and that we must be at its very heart. Here we perceive him suffering from the Grand Illusion. Far from influencing Europe and moulding it into a union nearer to our hearts' desire, we shall be sidelined – brushed aside by a group jealous of our past achievements and democratic government, once a model for the world.

Our fishermen and farmers have already had a taste of the Euro-State. I doubt whether one of them would ever vote for it. Spanish fishing boats in the Irish Sea! (Good heavens – it's enough to make Sir Francis quit the port of heaven and drum them up the Channel as he drummed them long ago!)

We are told that it is only a question of time before the pound gives way to the Euro. Yet to abolish the pound will destroy the quality of all our future lives. It will destroy London's eminence as a centre of world finance, a position in which it currently equals in importance the mighty power of Wall Street.

Sadly, this charismatic and talented young Prime Minister of ours will need close watching. He says one thing but does another. He is mesmerised by the awful power that has been placed in his hands and will use it to achieve objectives which, while he considers them good for Britain, will certainly destroy our nations and remove them from the world stage for ever. *We must stop him!*

It is true, is it not, that Scottish influence in our English Government is excessive and that some decidedly odd people are popping in and out of Number Ten? As Lord Acton said many years ago, all power corrupts. Mr Blair has demonstrated the truth of this by 'nobbling' the House of Lords and stuffing the House of Commons with his 'babes' and others.

May the day soon come when Mr Blair himself is transferred to the

House of Lords. Then he will find himself bereft of the power to damage all our futures.

Watch out too for The Three Marketeers:

Arthos Blair

Porthos Heseltine

Aramis Clarke

They want to place us in 'the heart of Europe' and at the *feet* of France, Germany, and the rest of the Brussels gang. When the promised Referendum comes, say NO, NO, NO!

CHAPTER 103

The European Union

The British people are drifting in a state of somnolism, and blissfully unaware, in many cases, toward the extinction of their nation as a major power. If they do not awaken soon – it will be too late and they will find that they have become mere provincial subjects in the eastern region of a monster Federation ruled by a rag-bag of unaccountable Commissioners, whose removal would be very difficult indeed.

They will have abolished the Houses of Parliament, already gravely weakened under the Blair Government. They will have exchanged *Habeas Corpus* for *Corpus Juris*, a very different means of protecting the individual.

They will have given up the ability to set their own taxes and interest rates. In other words, they will lose control of our economy.

They will lose control of their own armed forces and could be brought into some future conflict against the wishes of our people.

The gold reserves of The Bank of England have already been used to buy a sackful of Euros that we neither need nor desire.

Every aspect of all our lives is under threat. Ask our fishermen; ask our farmers. We are not even allowed to use our traditional weights and measures. More of this impertinent intrusion into our affairs is sure to follow.

Three very dangerous men are working behind the scenes to throw away a thousand years of liberty: that unholy trinity of Mr Kenneth Clark, Mr Michael Heseletine, and our Prime Minister, Mr A. Blair.

These men are not wicked. They fervently believe that Britain should, in Mr Blair's words, 'be at the Heart of Europe'. These clever men all suffer from the Politically Correct virus and they will prevail unless we stop them at Referendum time. They will delay that Referendum right until the last possible moment. They are working for a *fait accompli*! Watch them carefully over the coming months.

They suffer from the delusion that we can influence the EU and bring it to our ideas of democracy and business probity. They are weak in their knowledge of history and have scant regard for Britain's past. If we scrap the pound and join the EU, hook, line and sinker, we shall lose our identity, the eminence of London as a top world financial centre and we shall count for nothing in the councils of the world.

213

The Three Marketeers mentioned above fail to comprehend an irrefutable and profound truth: two of the main players in the EU, France and Germany, positively dislike us and are already working against our interests. Despite presidential embraces and handshakes, they have a mutual interest in our decline. The Germans, deep down in their psyche, hate us because twice this century we have frustrated their pan-European ambitions. The French dislike us because they feel humiliated by the fact that twice this century we have saved them from subjugation at the hands of their new-found 'friend' – strange bedfellows!

Voices in France demand that we rename Waterloo Station and Trafalgar Square! There are some who would accede to that.

I hope my countrymen and women will realise that being against EU membership is *not* being anti-European. We are Europeans and share with our continental nations the Greco-Roman Christian heritage which has shaped all our cultures and societies. We can, we must, cooperate with Europe as closely as possible in all fields but without any abject surrender of sovereignty.

At this moment Britain is in a free-fall of decline. All is not lost, for despite all the bad things going on in our society, the heart of this old country is as sound as ever and if we get it right at the next election, and especially if we get that vital referendum right, we shall recover.

Meanwhile, we can expect a sustained campaign by the Three Marketeers to frighten the electorate by dire warnings of mass unemployment and sanctions against us by the EU.

Do not be deceived! The EU needs us more that we need them, for the world is our oyster. If we work hard together, we can thrive and keep our rightful place as one of the world's great powers. We cannot do that unless we retain control of our own affairs.

Mr Blair controls much of the media; parliament and the BBC are under his tight control. Remember this when you hear horror stories about our fate if we fail to join the EU. So take his propaganda, and that of his cohorts, with the proverbial 'pinch of salt'.

Despite the break-up of the UK engineered by this government, we can still retain our English independence. Let William Pitt (1759-1806) speak again for us:

'England has saved herself by her exertions and will, as I trust, save Europe by her example.'

There is not much time, but we can do it if we keep cool heads and vote for sanity, justice and decent self-preservation.

We must not allow ourselves to be sidelined, brushed aside in Brussels.

We must not betray our dead in two Wars. They gave their lives for liberty, for all our tomorrows.

When the promised Referendum Day comes, vote NO! NO! NO!

Beware! Our Prime Minister is showing signs of becoming a (temporary) Euro-Sceptic! He fears the people's verdict on his normal anti-British stance.

CHAPTER 104

New Labour's Agenda!

Break up the United Kingdom

Abolish the Pound

Join the EU

Abolish Clause 28 (Local Government Act)

Encourage Homosexuality

Destroy our best schools (Read my lips, no selection!)

Abolish the Family

Damage our Armed Forces by forcing Women and Homosexuals on to HM Ships and into front-line combat units.

And, now a soldier can sue his CO!

New Labour's emblem? . . . THE DOME! (I prefer the Ex Royal Navy College just a few yards away from that ugly boil on the fair face of Greenwich).

CHAPTER 105

Women Priests

Recently the Archbishop of Canterbury 'ordained' twenty-two ladies as priests. A brief close-up of the assembled reverend ladies gave me a fright.

Does the Church really believe that any of the truly faithful could take these clerical amazons seriously? How silly, how comical they appeared in their Persil-white surplices with collars worn in reverse like their male brethren. Hugging one another, and in one case howling with laughter, they know little and care even less about how much damage they have done to the Apostolic Succession. In no great religion that I can think of are women accorded a sacramental role. Not one of the Apostles was a woman and no historical precedent exists for female priests in the mainstream religions. It may take as long as a century for the Anglican Church to recover from this schism. Just imagine: at the most sacred moment of the Holy Communion, the moment of Consecration, a male communicant might find himself distracted by his proximity to the beauty of a woman priest offering the chalice to his lips. Some ladies, left without a man, keep a poodle. Now, to compensate for their single state, there will be those who take, not the veil, but a curacy. Oh yes, some, no doubt, will take a husband too. For they have this in common with their male counterparts in the Anglican Communion, that they are not sworn to celibacy. I see some potential here for cupid to work his mischief! just at a time when the Church of England is facing ever-growing competition from Islam in Britain, she is plunged into conflict within by this foolish business of female priests. How sad it all is!

CHAPTER 106

Les Femmes, 1975 – A Lament!

She is pretty, but she's painted,
She is clean, yet she is tainted.
Her innocence lost when in slip and stockings,
Her avarice lives in a heart that is mocking.
She is motherhood with a 'fag' in her lips,
She leads men to shame when she swivels her hips.
She knows all the positions, she's read all the books.
She prefers supermarkets to churches and palaces,
Her talk is a medley of scandal and fallacies.
She cooks from a packet and not *Cordon Bleu*.
There is not much to say that is good about her
Yet when she lifts a finger – *you'll come running, sir*!

I wrote this at the time things were changing rapidly and the PC virus was bringing a new sort of woman into our society. I dedicate it to Mr Keith Waterhouse's Sharon and Tracey!

CHAPTER 107

Homosexuality

We are now a markedly homosexual country. I see real good in the fact that homosexuals no longer have to live, as in the days of my youth, in daily fear of being found out, ridiculed, ostracized or even sent to prison. Goodbye and good riddance to all that! At the same time homosexuals (I reject the highjacked word 'gay') have a clear duty to respect the feelings of the vast majority who find their activities repugnant. All of us should keep our sexual identity strictly private. To flaunt it in vulgar TV shows and in squalid radio programmes and press articles is more than we can reasonably be asked to tolerate. The homosexual infiltration of the media is out of all proportion to the numbers of homosexuals in our society.

Our Broadcasting and Press Complaints Officers have a job to perform here, and in general they are failing to do it. A friend of mine of thirty years, who is a household name as disc jockey, is homosexual. I am sure that not one those listening to his warm, jokey voice knows that it belongs to a life-long homosexual. I admire and respect that man.

I recall an animated lower deck debate on the subject of homosexuality which took place aboard the light cruiser, HMS *Calypso*. The discussions were often ribald and irreverent, with an occasional sensible comment thrown in by an old naval sage, but the whole debate was brought to a hilarious conclusion by a remark from an old sea dog of a Petty Officer, soon due to 'swallow the anchor' (leave the Service). 'Shipmates,' he declared, 'It's a biological absurdity.'

I confess, dear reader, that I am gay – especially when I have had a pint or two of local strong ale! However I am *never* homosexual. 'Gay' as a word has been highjacked by the politically correct.

CHAPTER 108

The Protestant Rebellion in England

Some theologians and historians see England as chosen by the Almighty to lead and sustain the Protestant revolution against Papal power, which in the 16th century was all-pervading. Two events in history seem to lend some credence to this theory: Henry VIII's break with Rome in 1531, following upon the Pope's refusal to allow him to divorce and re-marry, and the defeat of the Spanish Armada in 1588. Following on from this latter, England played a leading role in opening up the New World. She was a pioneer in introducing new concepts of liberty and of the sovereign dignity of the individual.

The defeat of the Armada may be ascribed to an astonishing combination of fine seamanship and extremely foul weather. In this it has something in common with Hitler's strange decision not to move against England at a time when she was standing alone, and to turn eastwards instead and declare war against Russia. Both events in history could be interpreted as signs of divine favour. After the Armada men said: *'Afflavit Deus et dissipati sunt'*, 'God blew and they were scattered'.

At this point Shakespeare's famous words from King John are highly relevant: 'Come the three corners of the world in arms, and we shall shock them. Naught shall make us rue if England to itself do rest but true!' *Today we should remember these words as never before!*

Big Bang!

Contemporary scientists claim to have confirmed the 'Big Bang' theory of the origin of our universe. They claim to have located the boundary of Space, the very end of the universe itself.

Tosh! What impertinence, what arrogance! These clever fellows resemble small boys tossing pebbles in the air on a beach. Do they not know that neither time nor space have any end? That the only reality is infinity, endless time and endless space? To these dimensions of infinity can be added the infinite nature of human love, a part of the same divine equation. We shall never know everything, and thank God for that!

Let our poet and eccentric, William Blake (1757 to 1827) have the last word here. We ought . . .

> To see a World in a Grain of Sand,
> And a Heaven in a Wild Flower,
> Hold Infinity in the palm of your hand
> And Eternity in an hour.

CHAPTER 110

Germans in the Ukraine

Some acts by human beings are so wicked as to be beyond forgiveness. A Russian War documentary records one such, and it needs no further comment. (Readers with delicate stomachs should turn the page at this point.)

Ample evidence exists of the fact that the treatment of civilians in the Ukraine at the hands of German troops was diabolically cruel (and this despite the fact that initially some Ukrainians actually welcomed the Germans as liberators from Moscow rule).

A group of starving Ukrainians approached a German army camp in their village and begged for food. 'Yes,' said the soldiers, 'We'll fetch you some. Wait here.' They returned with a parcel of excrement.

On the question of how civilians should be treated in the Ukraine, the German High Command was divided. Some high-ranking officers advocated a policy of cooperation and mutual support. Others – the prevailing group – insisted that these helpless people should be regarded as members of an inferior race and be treated with the utmost harshness. It is just possible that survivors of that German camp are now horrible old men walking the streets of their home towns as venerable old-age pensioners!

Chapter 111

American Indians

I recently taped a TV documentary on the history of the American Indians. Their story reveals the treachery and unscrupulous behaviour of the white man in the formative years of the United States. It is a record of broken treaties, lies and the despicable treatment of an ancient and (despite occasional lapses!) noble, people, whose culture and way of life was rooted in the law of nature and in the eternal mystery of the human predicament. The white man broke up Indian families and used every means, both devious and foul, to separate Indian children from their tribal history, language and customs. They herded these people into reservations or turned them into slaves. In my opinion, General Custer and his men got what they deserved. It is depressing to realise that many of the oppressors (brazen intruders into a land not given to them by God) were English Protestants descended from the first settlers. Nothing to be proud of here! The white man was the real savage. How strange that to millions of small boys (and many of their dads!) it is the Red Indian who stands today as the symbol of courage and nobility, not the 7th Cavalry!

CHAPTER 112

Israel and the Arabs

Homeward bound for Plymouth, we hove to outside Gibraltar harbour and sent our pinnace inshore to collect mail and newspapers.

The mail arriving in the mess is always an occasion of pleasure, but often of disappointment. Sailors crowd around the rating giving out the letters and he calls out the names of the lucky recipients. For the disappointed, there are words of consolation from shipmates. When I failed to get a letter, one of my more annoying shipmates used to say: 'Never mind, Ron, I'll let you read mine!' Or, worse still he would say, 'Cheer up, Ron, I'll write you a letter.'

On the day I have in mind, however, it was not the mail but the *Daily Express* which was the centre of attention. In those days (the 30's) that newspaper was a proud and patriotic paper with a full-size format, unlike the pathetic tabloid it is today. It spoke for Britain when we British could hold our heads high. On this day a whole page showed six British soldiers hanging, murdered by those evil cowards, Irgun Zwei Leumi, the Jewish terrorists.

Our soldiers were in Palestine to carry out the Mandate of the League of Nations and not as soldiers of Imperial Britain. This photograph on the front page cast a sombre cloud over the ship and there were no smiles or jokes as we proceeded to home waters.

Instead an atmosphere of suppressed fury prevailed, and that day, and that full-page picture, were etched into all our hearts.

Out of this vile crime was born the artificial sovereign state known today as Israel. Declarations and treaties do not change the truth, though they can and, in this case did, disregard it.

No Jewish person born in New York, Chicago, Moscow, Berlin or London, or anywhere else, can claim to be indigenous to the land of Palestine. Such a claim is, looked at with cool logic, tenuous indeed. Israel, supported chiefly by American arms and money, has assumed a false sovereignty over land that has belonged from time immemorial to the Arab peoples no less than to Hebraic ones. All this is not to deny that the Arabs have ruined their just cause by terrorism and war. They have paid for that.

After appalling suffering, the Jewish people were entitled to seek a safe haven, a land they could call their own. They should have tried to achieve that noble ideal in cooperation with the Arab states instead of presenting them with a *fait accompli*. The approach was wrong from the start.

Both peoples are Semites. It is hard to understand how a people so gifted, supreme in the arts and sciences, could brush aside and ignore the identity and national consciousness of the Arab States.

There are signs, small signs, that things are changing and that the good men in Tel Aviv are getting the message – cooperation is better than war. And, the Arabs too are grasping the nettle of recognising the divine right of the Jewish people to live in peace. Nevertheless, I cannot forget that awful day in Gibraltar nor will my shipmates. It seems there is no limit to human wickedness. Let then Jews and Arabs ponder the words of St John's Gospel, Chapter 13, Verse 34

'A new commandment I give unto you that ye love one another.'

And the Irish too!

CHAPTER 113

The Influence of the Press

The readers of the tabloid press sway in the wind like a field of ripe corn. (With acknowledgement to T.S. Elliot.)

CHAPTER 114

Two Englishmen

Twice a week for about ten or more years I exchanged greetings with a certain smartly dressed gentleman as we passed one another like ships passing in the night. We would exchange a cheerful 'Hello' or 'Nice Day' before continuing on our allotted paths. We never spoke or had even a brief conversation. We both knew we were strangers . . . and Englishmen.

One day, however, in simply gorgeous summer weather we sat on a seat in the park and talked! After the weather had been disposed of, we turned to politics and the state of the country. Then we exchanged our religious beliefs and both realised we were Arsenal supporters. He told me about his family and I told him about mine.

It was time for tea and we both realised we would have some explaining to do to our wives, for he had been to Sainsburys and I was heading there when our exchange of views began. So farewells were made and we parted.

A few days later our paths crossed again, but this time he just waved and said, 'I must rush', and I too was glad to see him go! The terrible truth dawned: We could not stand one another! We held identical views about everything so we had nothing to talk about! We were both bored to death. A brief encounter indeed!

CHAPTER 115

Disce Latinum – Learn Latin!
A Plea in Its Defence

I have been thinking recently about how to raise the profile of Latin in the school, so when I read that Professor Ron Dearing is advocating the re-introduction of Latin in state schools, I was cheered.

It has long been recognised that Latin is, apart from having an intrinsic value in its own right, enormously helpful to those learning to use their own language effectively. English is no longer traditionally taught from a grammatical standpoint, so pupils only learn about sentence structure and parts of speech from Latin.

At a recent seminar I attended, we agreed that we cannot assume knowledge in our pupils of any parts of speech with the possible exception of nouns and verbs. As for prepositions, conjunctions, participates and pronouns – even . . . !

Senior schools rely upon us in the prep schools to supply them with well-prepared pupils whose interest in the subject is still high. Some feel that they can help us by releasing some of their Common Entrance requirements, thus enabling us to broaden our syllabus to include more history and classical civilization. This is a very popular subject in the lower forms, where Achilles and Hector are household names, and their historic confrontation is regularly re-enacted in the playground.

Children must be shown how profoundly the civilizations of Greece and Rome have influenced our own. They are surprised when I tell them that there is Latin in every sentence we speak, and that about 60% of our English vocabulary is of Latin origin, just as they are amazed to discover that nearly all the subjects on the timetable are creations of the Greeks. Classical languages do not deserve that title 'dead'. They live on in us, for language is not a futile thing. It is a continuous process.

You may say, 'That is all very well, but what has it to do with the twentieth century? It is all in the past. It may be interesting but it is not relevant. We should be teaching Spanish or German.'

Well, first it is relevant, if the word means 'connected with the matter in hand'. The matter in hand is our culture. It is surely important to know who we are, where we came from, how Europe came to be what it is. I believe that whatever we do afterwards, we must begin with the Greeks and the Romans, for these great peoples were the twin pillars of our civilization, and by studying what we came from, we shall have a better idea of what we can become.

Mrs N. Porcheron (Our daughter, Nicolette)

CHAPTER 116

Deus Misereatur! – May God Have Mercy

The above quotation may serve to remind some how wickedly we have abused nature and mocked the natural law which is the Creator's law.

Consider some of the monstrous abuses, the arrogant and flagrant disobedience of man toward his Maker. Beware those who seek to clone living creatures, a grossly unnatural and wicked act. Even worse are those who encourage and seek to justify the disgusting employment of a syringe and a bucket to create a human being. Then there are those who pervert the natural order by genetically changing the God-given system of agriculture and supply of seeds. It is an act of open defiance of the natural order. We were never intended to eat genetically modified food and financial greed is the sole motive. The champions of GM crops claim that they will help arid areas of the world, but that is not their true objective.

We should also include in our list those foolish or wicked people who seek the destruction of the family and those who try to impart, under the guise of sex education, homosexual lifestyles to little children. And we must not omit those unholy ladies who wish to freeze their holy eggs.

If we continue along these lines, we shall forfeit God's mercy and then, one day, the threat of divine anger will become real.

Epilogue

This book is an octogenarian's last defiant shout at those who defile and spoil our beautiful world.

It is also an act of benediction for the blessings showered upon me, a lovely wife, dear children and many friends, both Naval and civilians. Ah, how could I forget my grandsons, Marcel and Pascal, twin sources of great happiness and much fun!

All this would never have come to pass if a certain drafting Commander had not removed me from the tragic Carrier HMS *Courageous* a few hours before she sailed for that dreadful rendezvous with U29.

At eighty-four I am haunted by those poignant words written by Sir Walter Raleigh the night before his execution.

> Even such is time that takes in trust
> Our youth, our joys, our all we have,
> And pays us but with age and dust.
> Who in the dark and silent grave,
> When we have wandered all our ways,
> Shuts up the story of our days.
> But from this earth, this grave, this dust,
> My God shall raise me up I trust
> Amen, Amen, Amen

I conclude with a brief *Apologia*: I hope that any wrong dates or place names will be pardoned in view of the fact that a time span of some 60 years lays bare the defects in a man's powers of recollection.

I wish not to hurt anyone's feelings. I attack only wrong ideas, not the people who hold them.

I hope we have shared a smile or two. Farewell and God be with you.

Ronald Bell